my life cycle

Maple Tree

CHERRY LAKE PRESS

Published in the United States of America by Cherry Lake Publishing Group
Ann Arbor, Michigan
www.cherrylakepublishing.com

Reading Adviser: Marla Conn, MS, Ed., Literacy specialist, Read-Ability, Inc.
Book Designer: Jennifer Wahi
Illustrator: Jeff Bane

Photo Credits: © AlessandroZocc/Shutterstock.com, 5; © Foisal Uddin/Shutterstock.com, 7; © dreamansions/Shutterstock.com, 9; © Ina Raschke/Shutterstock.com, 11; © SGr/Shutterstock.com, 13; © Maren Winter/Shutterstock.com, 15; © Melody Mellinger/Shutterstock.com, 17; © KrimKate/Shutterstock.com, 19; © LiuSol/Shutterstock.com, 21; © Elena Elisseeva/Shutterstock.com, 23; Cover, 2-3, 6, 16, 22, 24, Jeff Bane

Cherry Lake Press is an imprint of Cherry Lake Publishing Group.

Library of Congress Cataloging-in-Publication Data

Names: Gray, Susan Heinrichs, author. | Bane, Jeff, 1957- illustrator.
Title: Maple tree / Susan H. Gray ; illustrated by Jeff Bane.
Description: Ann Arbor, Michigan : Cherry Lake Publishing, 2021. | Series:
   My life cycle | Includes index. | Audience: Grades 2-3
Identifiers: LCCN 2020030599 (print) | LCCN 2020030600 (ebook) | ISBN
   9781534180000 (hardcover) | ISBN 9781534181717 (paperback) | ISBN
   9781534181014 (pdf) | ISBN 9781534182721 (ebook)
Subjects: LCSH: Maple--Life cycles--Juvenile literature.
Classification: LCC QK495.A17 G73 2021 (print) | LCC QK495.A17 (ebook) |
   DDC 583/.75--dc23
LC record available at https://lccn.loc.gov/2020030599
LC ebook record available at https://lccn.loc.gov/2020030600

Printed in the United States of America
Corporate Graphics

About the author: Susan H. Gray has a master's degree in zoology. She loves writing science books, especially about animals. Susan lives in Arkansas with her husband, Michael. Their neighborhood is full of maple trees.

About the illustrator: Jeff Bane and his two business partners own a studio along the American River in Folsom, California, home of the 1849 Gold Rush. When Jeff's not sketching or illustrating for clients, he's either swimming or kayaking in the river to relax.

I'm a maple tree seed. I have a special cover with a **papery** wing.

5

Why do some people call this a helicopter?

A seed like me is called a **samara**. I fall from a maple tree and spin to the ground.

I become covered with soil and dead leaves. Winter comes and goes.

When it warms up, I grow a tiny **root**. Next, my **shoot** pokes up. Then, leaves appear. I'm a **seedling** now.

Years pass, and I grow into a **sapling**. I'm not very tall. My **trunk** is skinny. But I sure look like a tree.

Later, flowers grow from my branches. My male flowers have **pollen**, but my female flowers do not.

15

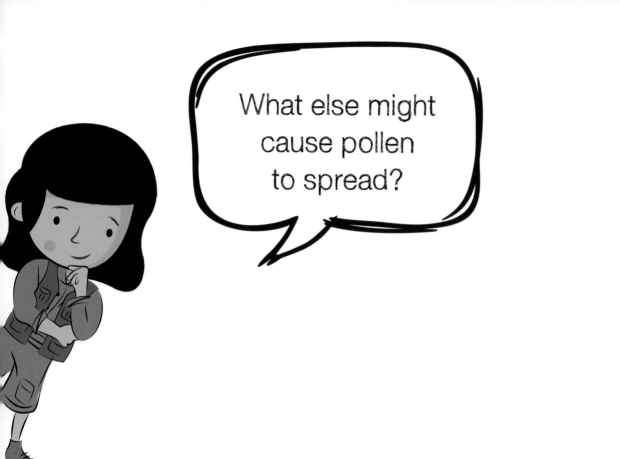

What else might
cause pollen
to spread?

Insects visit my flowers and
spread the pollen around.

Pollen lands on my female flowers. This makes them **develop** seeds.

Soon, samaras hang from my branches. One by one, they drop and spin to the ground.

What is your favorite thing about maple trees?

Winter comes and goes. It won't be long before little seedlings appear.

23

glossary

develop (dih-VEL-uhp) to grow

papery (PAY-puh-ree) thin and a little stiff, like paper

pollen (PAH-luhn) yellow powdery material produced by flowers

root (ROOT) the part of a plant or tree that grows under the ground

samara (SAM-er-uh) a winged seed

sapling (SAP-ling) a young tree

seedling (SEED-ling) a young plant that has grown from a seed

shoot (SHOOT) new plant growth coming up from the ground

trunk (TRUHNGK) the thick main part of a tree

index

Getting To Know...

Nature's Children

LOONS

Judy Ross

SCHOLASTIC INC.

New York   Toronto   London   Auckland   Sydney
Mexico City   New Delhi   Hong Kong   Buenos Aires

Facts in Brief

Classification of the Common Loon

Class: *Aves* (birds)
Order: *Gaviiformes* (loon-shaped birds)
Family: *Gaviidae* (loon family)
Genus: *Gavia*
Species: *Gavia immer*

World distribution.   Found with closely related species throughout the Northern Hemisphere.

Habitat.   Northern wilderness lakes in summer; ocean coasts and southern lakes in winter.

Distinctive physical characteristics.   Pointed bill; three-toed webbed feet set back toward its tail; in summer, white neck band, black back streaked with white; red eyes.

Habits.   Almost wholly aquatic but nests at water's edge; lives alone or in pairs; migrates southward for the winter; foot-propelled deep diver.

Diet.   Small fish, insects, frogs, weeds, crustaceans.

Published by Scholastic Inc.
90 Old Sherman Turnpike, Danbury, Connecticut 06816.

SCHOLASTIC and associated logos are trademarks and/or registered trademarks of Scholastic Inc.

ISBN: 0-7172-6717-2   Printed in the U.S.A.

Edited by: Elizabeth Grace Zuraw   *Photo Editor:* Nancy Norton
Photo Rights: Ivy Images   *Cover Design:* Niemand Design

Have you ever wondered . . .

Have you ever heard someone say, "You're as crazy as a loon"? Some people think that expression got started because of the loon's "ha-ha-ha" call, which sounds a bit like mad laughter. Because of that strange laughing call, loons once were thought to be crazy.

Today we know that there is nothing crazy about loons. But even though they're not crazy, they *are* remarkable in many ways. For instance, did you know that loons are such good underwater swimmers that they:

—could beat most fish in a race

—can swim when they are only a few hours old

—can sink out of sight while swimming?

In fact, this bird rarely sets foot on land except to lay its eggs. Curious about such an unusual creature? Let's find out more about this beautiful water-loving bird with an unforgettable voice.

With its distinctive white stripes and spots, a loon is easy to spot.

Water Babies

Loon chicks go for their first swim when they are only a few hours old, and in no time at all they're contentedly paddling around behind their parents. But loon babies are a bit like human babies; they get tired easily. For that reason a mother loon takes care not to swim too fast for her babies. And if the little ones get too tired, she will even let them scramble up onto her back where they can ride until they're rested and ready to swim again.

Because loons spend most of their lives in the water, it's important for the chicks to become strong swimmers. Fortunately, swimming seems to come naturally to loon chicks. After all, they come from a family of superb swimmers and divers.

A young loon always stays close to its mother. When tired, it may even hitch a ride on her back.

The Loon Family

There are four "cousins" in the loon family—
the Yellow-billed, Red-throated, Arctic, and
Common. Each has its own special *markings,*
distinctive patterns or colors of feathers. Can
you guess what's special about the Yellow-
billed Loon? Or about the Red-throated Loon?
Their names will give you the answer. The
Arctic Loon has a gray head and lives, as you
might have guessed, in the Arctic.

To find out more about the fourth cousin—
the Common Loon—turn the page.

*It's easy to spot a Red-throated Loon. Just
look for the patch of color on its throat.*

The Common Loon

Common Loons got their name because they are the loons we see most often. It's easy to tell the Common Loon from its cousins. In the spring and early summer, it has bright red eyes, a black-and-white checkerboard coat, and a thin "necklace" of white markings around its neck.

In late summer, the Common Loon *molts*, or sheds its feather coat, before growing a new one. In its place, the loon grows a drab gray winter outfit, and its white necklace almost disappears. Against this gray coat, its eyes look more brown than red.

If you were to see a male and female loon swimming together, you wouldn't be able to tell them apart. Unlike many birds, both male and female loons have the same markings.

A loon's bill is long, sharp, and pointed—useful features for fishing.

Two Homes

The Common Loon has two homes. In summer it lives on northern and wilderness lakes in parts of North America, Iceland, and Europe. But when its home lake freezes in late fall, the loon must *migrate,* or travel, south. If it were to stay where it is, a covering of ice would cut the loon off from the fish it eats, and it would starve.

Some North American loons spend winters on the ocean where there is salt water, which does not freeze. Others winter as far south as California and Florida.

A list of a loon's favorite foods wouldn't be complete without pickerel, bass, and other fish—even frogs.

Built for Swimming

When you want to go for a swim, you put on a bathing suit and maybe even a bathing cap, swim fins, and floats. A loon doesn't need any special equipment to go swimming. Its body is perfectly suited to live in the water.

The loon's body is torpedo-shaped so it can cut through the water smoothly and easily. To propel itself, the loon has big *webbed feet,* feet with toes joined together by flaps of skin. And the feet are set back toward its tail. Having its feet at the back of its body gives the loon extra paddle power. When a loon swims on the surface, it uses its feet like a miniature paddle wheel to push itself forward. For under-water swimming the loon thrusts itself forward, using its feet like the propeller on a boat.

The loon's feathers also are ideal for life in the water. They grow so close together that no water can get through them. Besides water-proofing the loon, the feathers also trap air, which helps the loon float high in the water— even if several chicks are hitching a ride.

Opposite page: *Loons often rear up in the water, flap their wings, stretch their necks, shake their heads, then settle back down.*

Underwater Acrobats

The loon is a superb diver and underwater swimmer. It dips, dives, and soars underwater as if it were flying. It even "flaps" its wings underwater for a burst of extra speed or to help it change directions quickly.

Loon

To see a loon dive you must watch closely. If you blink you might miss it. The loon plunges forward with its neck arched and pushes itself down with its strong feet. It dives so quickly and quietly that it hardly leaves a ripple behind on the water's surface.

Duck

A good game is trying to figure out where the loon will resurface after a dive. It can swim great distances underwater—as far as a city block—in less than a minute. Loons are deep divers, too. A loon has been caught in a fisherman's net 240 feet (70 meters) below the surface!

Notice how much farther back a loon's legs are set than a duck's.

A mother loon may not dive when she senses danger. Instead, she may dance on the water to draw attention away from her nest.

17

The Loon on Land

The loon is a graceful and powerful swimmer, but on land it's so awkward that you might think it has two left feet. Because the loon's legs are toward the back of its body and its feet are large and webbed, it has trouble walking on land. Running is almost impossible. Sometimes a loon loses its balance altogether and flops over onto its belly. Then it must flap its wings wildly to get up again. If it is tired, it might give up and push itself along the ground on its belly.

The loon's clumsiness on land may be amusing to watch, but it can be a problem for the bird. Loons can't escape if a hungry mink or lynx or other loon enemy chases it. To avoid *predators,* animals that hunt other animals for food, loons go on land only when they are nesting. Even then, they build their nests at the edge of the water so that they can hop in and swim off if a predator comes near.

Opposite Page:
Being clumsy walkers on land, loons wisely build their nests as near to water as possible.

Now You See It, Now You Don't

A swimming loon has a special trick that allows it almost to disappear when it is frightened. It can sink part way into the water so that less of its body can be seen. To do this, a loon squeezes its feathers together to get rid of air trapped between them. And it forces the air out of its lungs. Without all that air to keep it afloat, it slowly sinks lower into the water.

Nicknamed the "Great Northern Diver," the Common Loon can dive deeper than any other flying bird.

A Fine Fisher

Have you ever gone fishing? If you have, you probably sat and sat for a long time waiting for a fish to nibble on your bait. What a pity people can't fish the way a loon does. Instead of waiting for the fish to come to it, the loon jumps into the water and goes after the fish.

The loon dives for fish and traps them in its bill. A small fish is usually eaten underwater in one big gulp, but bigger fish are brought up to the surface before being swallowed whole. The loon eats mostly small fish and minnows.

Sometimes, when a loon is looking underwater for its next meal, it munches on other underwater goodies such as frogs, weeds, and even clams.

Superb swimmers, loons can stay underwater for a minute or longer as they fish for meals.

Opposite page:

*Loon takeoffs and
landings are bumpy
adventures.*

Take Off—Splash Down

Birds that spend a lot of time in the air cannot
afford to carry around any extra weight. Their
bones are filled with tiny pockets of air so that
they weigh less. But the loon does not have
these air-filled bones. This bird spends most of its
life in or under the water where its heavier bones
are useful.

What happens when the heavier-boned loon
tries to take off? It really has to work at it. To
get airborne, a loon needs a long water runway.
It heads into the wind with its feet running
madly on the water's surface. It half flies and
half runs until it builds up enough speed to
take off—it's quite a job!

Once in the air, the loon looks hunchbacked.
Its big webbed feet trail out behind its short
tail, and its neck reaches downward as if it
were looking at the water below all the time.

A loon cannot land gracefully either. The
loon zooms in low over the water, almost as if
it cannot brake in the air, and belly flops down
onto its breast. Then it skids through the water,
sending spray everywhere.

Loon Talk

Loons live alone or in pairs, rather than in large flocks. On a small lake you'll usually find only one loon couple. On a larger lake there might be other pairs, but each pair will live in a separate bay. By spreading out in this way, the loons can be sure of finding enough food.

Even though loons rarely visit each other, they often "talk" to each other. When one loon cries out, another will sometimes answer from a faraway bay. This makes it sound as if the call is being echoed all across the lake.

The loon is well known for its distinctive calls. It has a mad-sounding, laughing "ha-ha-ha" call and a haunting wail that sounds like "Who-who-Who-Who-o-o-o." This lonely sounding call can often be heard at dusk or when a storm is approaching.

The haunting cry of a loon is so unusual that once you hear it, you'll never forget it.

Mating Dance

Loons are believed to choose a *mate* for life. They do this by performing a special dance during *mating season*, the time of year when animals come together to produce young. The mating dance looks like a beautiful water ballet. Treading water side by side, two courting loons will suddenly take off and race wildly across the water. At other times, they swim slowly toward each other.

When their bodies touch, they both stretch their bills up into the air.

During mating season, loons perform a graceful dance.

A Waterside Nest

In early June, the loon pair choose a place for the female to lay the eggs. Often the pair returns to a place they have used before. If they can't, they look for a rocky point of land or an island—always near water. Sometimes they use a clump of floating weeds and plants as a ready-made nest, and sometimes they even lay the eggs on the top of a muskrat house!

The mother loon lays two eggs that are about twice as big as chicken eggs. Loon eggs are greenish or brownish and speckled to blend in with the grasses and plants around the nest area. This *camouflage,* or blending in with surroundings, helps hide the eggs from hungry egg-eaters such as otters, raccoons, and skunks.

Both mother and father loons take turns caring for the eggs. If the parents ever need to leave the nest, they return very quickly.

Protective Parents

Sometimes loon parents pull bits of weeds and grass over the eggs to make them more difficult for predators to find. Then the mother and father loon take turns sitting on the eggs to keep them safe and warm.

It takes about 30 days for the eggs to *hatch,* or produce a baby chick. Loon parents must be constantly on the lookout for danger. If an enemy comes near the nest, the mother and father loon take to the water and swim away so that the location of their eggs is kept a secret. But there are other dangers besides predators. The eggs may be swept off their nest by the rush of water from a passing motorboat. Or they may be destroyed by the high waves of a bad storm.

A loon parent turns an egg to be sure that all sides of it stay warm.

Hatch Day

When the little chicks break out of their shells, they are wet and sticky and look as if they are all beaks and feet. Their soft *down* feathers are a dark brown-black. Down is the name for a bird's soft, fluffy feathers. The dark coloring helps the loon chick blend in with the nest area so that it cannot be seen by hungry predators.

In just a few hours, the chicks are ready to leave the nest for good and begin their life in the water.

After the hard work of cracking out of its egg, this loon chick is taking a rest. But within just hours, it will be out of the nest and in the water for good.

Growing Up

Loon chicks learn to swim and dive by imitating their mother and father. The loon parents keep a close watch over their youngsters. They bring the chicks small fish to eat until the chicks can fish for themselves. Sometimes, instead of fish, the chicks eat a green salad made of water plants. When they have learned to swim and dive, the chicks start to fish for their own food.

Loon chicks eat a lot and grow quickly. By the end of summer, their fluffy down molts and they grow a new coat of gray feathers. These are flying feathers, and once they have grown in, the young loons begin to learn how to fly. By late September they are flying confidently and are almost fully grown.

With their gray flying feathers growing in, these baby loons will soon begin to learn how to fly. Loon chicks are at least ten weeks old before their flying lessons begin.

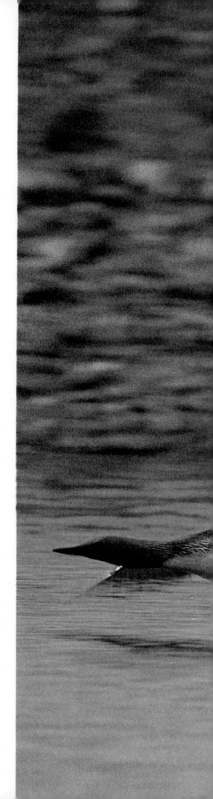

The Flight South

Loons must leave their home lake when it ices over in late fall. They head south until they find a lake without ice, where they can still fish. When this lake freezes, they must fly still farther south in search of another open lake. Pushed farther and farther south by the weather, the loons hop from lake to lake. Finally they reach an ocean coast or a southern lake where the water never freezes. Here they spend the winter, often in small groups.

Once in the air, loons are strong fliers, but they need to patter a long distance before becoming airborne. They cannot take flight from land.

42

On Their Own

The loons begin making their way back north in the early spring. As soon as the ice breaks up on a lake or river, the loons are there. Flying north lake by lake, they return to their summer homes.

The young loons don't return to where they were hatched. Their parents are probably already there. Instead the youngsters look for a new lake or river where they will have enough food and a good choice of *nesting sites,* suitable places to build a nest.

Some loons arrive at the nesting ground with a mate. Others find a mate there. Once partners have been found, the young loons are ready to start families of their own.

Loons sometimes are called divers *because of their skill in diving for fish to eat. True water birds, loons spend little time on land.*

Words To Know

Camouflage Feathers, coloring, or other features that blend in with an animal's surroundings so that it can avoid being seen.

Down A bird's soft, fluffy feathers.

Hatch To produce young from an egg.

Markings Distinctive patterns or colors of fur or feathers.

Mate To come together to produce young. Either member of an animal pair is also the other's mate.

Mating season The time of year when animals come together to produce young.

Migrate To move from one place to another in search of food.

Molt To shed feathers before growing new ones.

Nesting site A place to build a nest.

Predator An animal that hunts other animals for food.

Webbed feet Feet with toes that are joined together by flaps of skin.

Loons live mostly in the northern parts of the world.
They are sometimes mistaken for geese or ducks,
but loons' thick necks, pointed bills, and awkward
movements on land set them apart from those
other water birds.

Index

PHOTO CREDITS
Cover: Bill Ivy. **Interiors:** *Valan Photos:* Wayne Lankinen, 4, 27; Stephen J. Krasemann, 8, 42; Brian Milne, 14; Esther Schmidt, 20; Pam Hickman, 34. /Wayne Lankinen, 7, 16, 32, 40, 45. /*Network Stock Photo File:* Ken Carmichael, 11, 37, 46; Jacob Formsma, 30-31. /Bill Ivy, 13, 23, 24, 29. /James Richards, 39.

Getting To Know...

Nature's Children

BLACK BEARS

Caroline Greenland

SCHOLASTIC INC.

New York Toronto London Auckland Sydney
Mexico City New Delhi Hong Kong Buenos Aires

Facts in Brief

Classification of the Black Bear

    Class: *Mammalia* (mammals)
    Order: *Carnivora* (meat-eaters)
    Family: *Ursidae* (bear family)
    Genus: *Ursus*
    Species: *Ursus americanus*

World distribution. Exclusive to North America. Related species widely distributed throughout most of the Northern Hemisphere.

Habitat. Forest regions, swamps, and dense bushland.

Distinctive physical characteristics. Smallest of the North American bears; usually black with tan muzzle and white patch under throat; claws are comparatively short and curved.

Habits. Primarily solitary; fast runner; skilled tree climber; sleeps deeply for most of the winter; wanders far for food.

Diet. Plant life: roots, leaves, berries, grasses, fruit, and acorns; small mammals, frogs, fish, insects; honey.

Published by Scholastic Inc.
90 Old Sherman Turnpike, Danbury, Connecticut 06816.

SCHOLASTIC and associated logos are trademarks and/or registered trademarks of Scholastic Inc.

ISBN: 0-7172-6717-2   Printed in the U.S.A.

Edited by: Elizabeth Grace Zuraw   *Photo Editor:* Nancy Norton
Photo Rights: Ivy Images   *Cover Design:* Niemand Design

Have you ever wondered . . .

Do you remember your very first Teddy Bear? It probably was soft and furry with little round ears, a black button nose, and a squishy body just made for cuddling.

Children have had Teddies ever since the beginning of the century, when United States President Teddy Roosevelt saved a Black Bear cub from being killed. A toymaker, charmed by this story, decided that a bear would make a nice, huggable plaything for a child and created the first Teddy Bear.

Baby Black Bears look as huggable as toy Teddy Bears—but watch out! Their mother may be lurking nearby, ready to chase off anyone who comes near her babies.

Black Bears are experts at climbing and balancing. Even the babies can quickly scoot up a tree to hide from an enemy—or just hang out.

Bundles of Fun

Summertime is playtime for baby Black Bears. While their mother looks on, the babies, called *cubs,* chase butterflies, play tag, and wrestle with each other.

If a hungry cougar or another bear comes too close, the mother shoos the cubs up the nearest tree. Then, growling fiercely, she scares off the intruder.

When the danger has passed, the mother calls to her babies, and they come shimmying down to the ground to play some more.

Once a cub is shooed up a tree by its mother, it may stay up for 20 hours or more until she signals that it's safe to come down again.

Bear Territory

Black Bears are the most common of the North American bears, and compared to their relatives, the Brown and Polar Bears, Black Bears are also the smallest. They can be found across most of North America, up into Alaska, and even as far south as Mexico. Black Bears prefer to live in thickly wooded areas or dense brushland, near a creek, stream, or lake.

The Black Bears that live in North America have cousins in Asia. Smaller than the North American Black Bears, these Asiatic Black Bears prefer to live in mountains and forests.

Black Bear

Brown Bear

Polar Bear

The Bear Facts

Male bears are called *boars*. Black Bear boars
weigh about 375 pounds (170 kilograms),
which means it would take two fully grown
men on one end of a seesaw to balance a Black
Bear on the other end. Female bears, called
sows, weigh slightly less than the males.

*The shaded area
shows where Black
Bears are found.*

Many-colored Coat

Don't be fooled by their name. Not all Black Bears are black. Most are black with a brownish muzzle and a white throat patch or other white chest markings. But some Pacific Coast Black Bears are almost white; others are bluish, a color created by black fur mixed with gray hairs. Cinnamon-colored Black Bears are quite common in Western Canada and the United States. In other areas, Black Bears may be brown, dark brown, or even blue-black. And sometimes—although it's unusual—a mother has cubs of different colors in the same *litter,* the group of animals born at the same time.

Whatever their color, all Black Bears have long, coarse fur that is not at all soft and cuddly like a Teddy Bear's coat. Every spring Black Bears shed their winter coat and grow a lighter-weight summer coat.

This Black Bear is easy to tell because of the color of its fur. But Black Bears can also be brown, blue-black, and even white.

Scents, Sounds, and Sights

The Black Bear uses its long snout to sniff out other animals as well as a good supply of food, such as a patch of berries. To get a really big noseful of smells, a bear often stands on its hind legs with its snout in the air.

A bear's rounded, furry ears also are useful. The animal's keen sense of hearing means that nothing or no one can sneak up on the bear without being noticed.

It's a good thing that a bear can smell and hear so well, because its eyesight is poor. In fact, a Black Bear has difficulty recognizing objects by sight. And Black Bears are color-blind. This means they see only in shades of black, gray, and white. They cannot see colors.

A long snout helps make smell the Black Bear's sharpest sense.

Bear Talk

If you were to overhear two Black Bears "talking," you'd hear a strange combination of growls, whines, and sniffs. Although you might have a problem understanding this kind of communication, Black Bears don't. For instance, if a baby bear hears its mother make a sharp "woof-woof" sound, it knows danger is nearby. And every mother Black Bear knows that a baby-like cry from one of her little ones means the cub is in trouble—or hungry.

A gentle sniff is one way Black Bears communicate.

Getting Around

Unlike many animals, but like you, bears put their whole foot, including their heel, on the ground when they walk. Because they do this with all four feet, they have an awkward, lumbering walk. But if a bear is in a hurry, it can reach speeds of up to 35 miles (55 kilometers) per hour. A running bear looks a bit like a huge, black beachball bouncing through the woods.

Swimming is second nature to a Black Bear. It can "dog-paddle" across small lakes or rushing rivers with ease. And when a Black Bear climbs out of the water, it shakes itself dry like a big shaggy dog.

Black Bear paw prints

A bear usually travels along the same routes over and over again within its territory.

Front paw

The strong curved claws of the Black Bear work much like grappling hooks when it is climbing a tree.

Going Up

If you were in a tree-climbing contest with a Black Bear, the bear would probably win. A Black Bear climbs trees to escape danger or to take a good look around for food. To help it climb, it has five hooked claws on each paw. The bear hugs the trunk with its front paws and hooks its strong, curved claws into the bark. Then it pulls itself up with its front paws and pushes with its back paws. The bear does this so quickly that it looks as if it has leaped up the tree like an agile cat. But unlike cats, bears cannot pull in their claws. A bear's claws are always out and ready for action.

Coming Down

The Black Bear comes down a tree tail first, often dropping the last yards (meters) to the ground. Although you might be shaken up if you made such a sudden landing, the Black Bear doesn't even seem to notice. It just picks itself up and ambles off on its way.

Home Ground

Adult Black Bears keep out of each other's way most of the time. Each bear stakes out a *territory,* or area, that has enough food to keep it alive and healthy. In summer, when there are lots of green plants and berries, a bear's territory may be only about one square mile (three square kilometers). But in spring, when plants are just beginning to grow and food is scarce, the bear's territory may be ten times as big.

A Black Bear gives notice to other bears to stay away from its territory by posting "Stay Out" warnings. To do this, the bear stands on its hind legs beside a tree and makes claw marks on the bark. Any bears that come along see these claw marks and know they are entering an area that belongs to another bear. They can even tell the size of the bear whose territory they have wandered into. How? The higher the claw marks, the bigger the bear.

To mark off its territory, a Black Bear makes claw scratches on the bark of trees in the area.

Hungry as a Bear

When you think of a bear, do you think of a ferocious meat-eating animal? Bears do eat meat, but they also eat plants. That is why they are called *omnivores,* animals that eat both meat and plants.

The Black Bear is not a picky eater. In fact, it will eat almost anything that's available. Most of its diet is made up of plants, roots, grains, and fruit. The bear has very flexible lips and a long tongue that makes berry-picking easy. Favorite fruits include blueberries, strawberries, and apples, but bears also munch on nuts such as acorns, hazelnuts, and beechnuts.

In spring, Black Bears that live near the coast dine on migrating salmon. A Black Bear also will eat any meat it finds, but it won't normally kill another animal for food unless it is easy *prey.* Prey is an animal hunted by another animal for food.

Ambling through its territory, a Black Bear is ever watchful for insects, fruits, nuts, and other foods along the way.

A Black Bear also loves honey, but did you know that it likes to eat bees, too? Also high on its list of favorites are ants, grasshoppers, termites, and wasps. A bear's thick coat helps protect it from being stung by angry wasps and bees.

Tough Teeth

To chew up all the different kinds of foods it eats, a Black Bear has different kinds of teeth. Sharp, pointed, meat-cutting teeth for catching prey are in the front of the bear's mouth. Further back, broad, flat teeth called *molars* work like a potato masher to grind up tough plant fibers so that the bear can digest them more easily.

The Black Bear, famous for its sweet tooth, often pokes its nose into tree hollows looking for beehives and honey.

Bears Alone and Together

During the summer and fall, a Black Bear is out from dusk to dawn searching for food and eating as much as possible. It needs to put on a good layer of fat in preparation for the long winter. Then food will be hard to find, and the bear will need to live on its stored fat.

Summer is also the only time adult bears are likely to be seen together. That's because summer is *mating season,* the time of year during which animals come together to produce young. Once a bear finds a mate, the two spend a short time together—then they go their separate ways again.

During late summer, you might see a bear couple heading for a picnic of berries and other tasty treats.

Opposite page:
Bears often gather dead leaves and grass and chewed-off sticks as cozy bedding for their dens.

Getting Ready for Winter

When the temperature falls and food becomes scarce, a Black Bear searches for a *den*, an animal home, where it will sleep for the winter. Finding a warm, dry den is especially important for a mother Black Bear that is about to have a family. Long before the first snowfall, she begins to inspect caves, hollow logs, and overturned stumps. When she finds a safe and dry spot, she covers the floor of her winter home with moss, leaves, and grasses to make a snug nursery for her family.

Male bears are not nearly as fussy about their dens. They usually wait for the first snowfall before they even start looking for a winter home. By this time, the females have moved into all the best spots, but this doesn't seem to bother the males. If there is no den available, a male simply lies down in the shelter of an overturned stump and waits for the snow to fall. As the snow piles up around him, his body warmth melts the snow closest to him, leaving the rest to form a custom-made igloo around him.

A Long Winter's Sleep

Black Bears in northern areas may nap for up to six months in winter. Bears in warmer regions, where food is available year-round, do not need to sleep for so long. Black Bears are not true *hibernators,* they don't go into a kind of heavy and very deep winter sleep. A Black Bear may wake up and even leave its den if the weather is warm enough. When it gets cold again, the bear goes back to its den to snooze some more.

During this long winter's sleep, the bear's breathing and heart rate slow down. This means that the bear needs less energy. Instead of having to eat food for energy, it can live on its stored fat.

When a Black Bear wakes up in the spring, it is hungry and cranky and its stomach has shrunk because it has not eaten for so long. The first thing it does is look for food and water. Soon the bear's stomach will be full of new plant shoots and tree buds and the bear will be getting back to its roly-poly self.

A Surprise for Mother

Sows usually give birth to their tiny cubs in January or February, every other year. Mother bears in the North may be fast asleep in their snug dens when their babies are born. Just think of the surprise the mother bear gets when she wakes up and finds she is sharing her den with her new family!

Often there are two cubs, but sometimes there may be as many of five. Newborn Black Bear cubs are about the size of small squirrels. Their eyes are tightly shut, and they don't have any hair or teeth. They spend their first five weeks snuggling close to their mother and *nursing,* drinking milk from her body.

Overleaf:
A mother bear is seldom far from her cubs. She has many lessons to teach them before they'll be ready to go off on their own.

If these cubs were to smile, you might be able to see their milk teeth, or "baby teeth." Their permanent teeth don't start to grow until the cubs are nearly three months old.

Round and Round

When they first start to walk, the small cubs have strong front legs, but their back legs are weak and wobbly and drag behind them. The cubs can't crawl in a straight line. Instead, they usually just go round and round in circles! But that's a good thing. It means they never get far away from their mother, who might be fast asleep and unable to keep an eye on them.

A cub gets its first look at the outside world when it is about three months old.

*Climbing on its mother's back is more
than just fun for a cub. It's cozy, too. Her
fur is coarse, but also thick and warm.*

Padded Playground

Cubs start to grow a fine coat of soft fur when they are a week old. And they are able to see their mother for the first time at six weeks, when their eyes first open—but they are still very wobbly on their feet. Perhaps this is why they spend a lot of time climbing all over their mother, using her warm, furry body as a handy playground.

Bear School

The cubs are only puppy-sized when they leave the den for the first time in mid-April, so their mother keeps a close eye on them at all times. She is gentle and patient but quite strict with her cubs.

By watching their mother throughout their first year, the cubs learn all the skills a bear needs to survive. They learn how to find the right kinds of food, how to look for shelter from bad weather, and what animals to avoid—for example, cougars, lynxes, Grizzly Bears, and adult Black Bears.

Overleaf:
Two young cubs follow their mother across a beaver dam.

Weepy Wanderer

If a cub wanders off and gets lost, it cries and whines until its mother tracks it down. The mother uses her nose to nudge the wanderer gently back to the group. A crying cub is an upset cub. When a cub is content it purrs rather like a kitten.

If danger approaches, a mother bear hustles her cubs up a tree for safety. But often the playful youngsters climb trees just for the fun of it. They play tag with each other high in the trees and sunbathe on any convenient branch. In stormy weather, the bears take shelter in evergreen trees, using the overhanging branches as an umbrella to keep them dry.

Bears usually are *solitary,* they prefer living alone. But sometimes two mother bears travel together with their cubs. The females then share the task of cub-sitting, giving one of the mothers a chance to sleep or eat in peace.

Baby Black Bears look cute and cuddly, but like all wild animals, they don't make good pets.

On Their Own

The cubs curl up in a den and sleep away their first winter with their mother. Their survival lessons start up again in spring and continue until summer when the mother bear starts looking for another mate. At this point the *yearlings,* the name for animals that are a year old, are as big as St. Bernard dogs. They go on without their mother, but they often stay with a brother or sister for the rest of the summer. The cubs may even share a den that winter.

The following spring, the young bears go their separate ways, putting their newly learned survival skills to the test. But strong bonds have developed between them. If they meet later in their lives, they will be quite friendly toward each other.

Bears born in the same litter develop strong bonds with each other.

Put to the Test

The second year is the most difficult for a young Black Bear. Still small in size and inexperienced, it must find a territory with enough food to keep it healthy. And it must avoid larger bears, without the help of warning woofs from its mother. If it has learned its lessons well, a wild Black Bear will live to be ten to fifteen years old and have several families of its own.

Words To Know

Boar   A male bear.

Cub   The name for the young of various animals, including the Black Bear.

Den   An animal home.

Hibernation   A kind of heavy sleep that some animals take in the winter, during which their breathing and heart rates slow, and their body temperatures go down.

Hibernator   An animal that goes into hibernation for the winter.

Litter   A group of animal brothers and sisters born together.

Mate   To come together to produce young. Either member of an animal pair is also the other's mate.

Mating season   The time of year when animals come together to produce young.

Molars   Broad, flat teeth along the cheeks in the mouth that help grind up plant fibers.

Nurse   To drink milk from a mother's body.

Omnivore   An animal that eats both plants and meat.

Prey   An animal hunted by another animal for food.

Solitary   Being or living alone.

Sow   A female bear.

Territory   An area that an animal, or a group of animals, lives in and often defends from other animals of the same kind.

Yearling   An animal that is a year old.

Index

PHOTO CREDITS

Cover: Bill Ivy. **Interiors:** *Ivy Images:* Alan & Sandy Carey, 4, 14, 31, 38; Robert McCaw, 10, 19; Norman R. Lightfoot, 16; Patrick M. Collins, 23. /*Valan Photos:* Wayne Lankinen, 7, 13, 42; Hälle Flygare, 34-35; Esther Schmidt, 40-41. /Duane Sept, 20. /*Lowry Photo:* William Lowry, 24, 29. /Tim Fitzharris, 27. /Len Rue J₁ 32. /*Eco-Art Productions:* Norman Lighfoot, 37. /Barry Ranford, 45.

KAREN BLUMENTHAL

SIX DAYS IN OCTOBER

THE STOCK MARKET CRASH OF 1929

A WALL STREET JOURNAL BOOK

ATHENEUM BOOKS FOR YOUNG READERS

NEW YORK   LONDON   TORONTO   SYDNEY   SINGAPORE

TO DAD AND PAPPA, WHO TAUGHT ME ABOUT STOCKS

Atheneum Books for Young Readers

An imprint of Simon & Schuster Children's Publishing Division

1230 Avenue of the Americas, New York, New York 10020

Book design by Lauren Monchik

The text for this book is set in Bembo.

Printed in the United States of America

10 9 8 7 6 5 4 3 2

Library of Congress Cataloging-in-Publication Data

Blumenthal, Karen.

Six days in October : the stock market crash of 1929 / written by Karen Blumenthal.

p. cm.

Includes bibliographical references (p.) and index.

Summary: A comprehensive review of the events, personalities, and mistakes behind the Stock Market Crash of 1929, featuring photographs, newspaper articles, and cartoons of the day.

ISBN 0-689-84276-7

1. Stock Market Crash, 1929—Juvenile literature. 2. New York Stock Exchange—History—Juvenile literature. 3. United States—Economic conditions—1918-1945—Juvenile literature. 4. Depressions—1929—United States—Juvenile literature. 5. Depressions—1929—Juvenile literature. [1. Stock Market Crash, 1929. 2. New York Stock Exchange—History. 3. United States—Economic conditions—1918-1945. 4. Depressions—1929.] I. Title.

HB3717 1929.B58 2002

332.64'273—dc21   2001046360

CONTENTS

———◆———

INTRODUCTION

THE YEARS AFTER the First World War were a golden age for many Americans. The 1920s didn't just sing with the rhythms of jazz, or swing with the dancing of the Charleston; they roared with the confidence and optimism of a prosperous era.

For most of the decade, jobs were plentiful and paychecks grew steadily. Mass production and innovation helped make many items widely available and affordable. Automobiles became cheaper, faster, and more comfortable. Fledgling airlines began to carry a few passengers from city to city. Electric refrigerators and washing machines freed women from some household chores. Department stores and grocery chains expanded, offering a greater selection and lower prices than neighborhood markets.

As movies talked for the first time, radio brought instant news and entertainment into living rooms, spreading the word about the many things money could buy. A new industry, advertising, advised Americans that they needed toothpaste, mouthwash, and ready-made clothing.

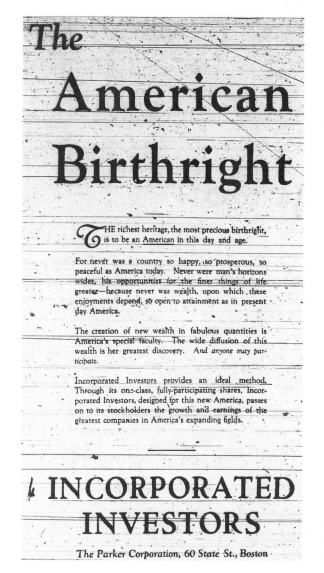

Brokerage houses advertised in newspapers and popular magazines to woo new investors. This August 1929 ad enticed readers with its claim that wealth was easily attainable for any American.

Young women, energized from winning the long fight for the right to vote, traded their heavy, long dresses for short, slim styles. They cut their hair short like the boys', and dared to wear makeup. Many women began to handle their own money.

With all the attention on buying and consumer goods, businessmen became widely admired public figures. The powerful men who ran the nation's largest banks, car companies, and electric utilities became national celebrities.

Money became the sign of success—though very few people were truly wealthy. Most working Americans made just a few thousand dollars a year and worked six days a week. But those who could save some money for a down payment and spare a few dollars more from each paycheck could buy one of Henry Ford's cars or a house in the suburbs on the partial-payment plan.

The New York Stock Exchange building, as seen by an artist in 1929. Here, at the corner of Broad and Wall streets in downtown Manhattan, was America's financial center.

Amid all the affluence, the average man saw one way that he, too, could become rich. On Wall Street, a narrow little road in New York City, magical things were said to happen to money. Men told coworkers about it, women told their sisters, neighbors told neighbors. Those who could scrape together a few hundred dollars—or even better, a few thousand dollars—could buy stocks, pieces of paper that represented a small ownership in a company. For much of the 1920s, stocks soared in value. People clever enough to buy them could end up with more

3

money than they ever imagined. Someone who had the foresight to buy $10,000 of General Motors stock in 1920 would have seen the investment grow to more than $1.5 million by 1929.

Unfortunately, few people had that kind of cash or insight—or luck. Many investors never made money in the market, or at least not very much. And there weren't all that many stock investors to start with. Out of 121 million people, probably just 1.5 million to 3 million of them owned stocks—just one or two out of every 100 Americans.

Still, as stock prices climbed higher and higher in 1928 and 1929, Americans were captivated by the idea of making money in such a fast and fantastic way. Newspapers listed daily stock prices. Radio broadcasts gave the day's stock-market highlights.

The fascination with wealth drew many more people than had ever before gambled their savings in such a risky and unpredictable place as the stock market. Their zeal was supported and encouraged by some of the nation's most respected leaders. As stock prices seemed to climb to the sky and beyond, these prominent men began to chase after wealth themselves. Executives who had spent their lives building solid reputations cut secret deals in pursuit of their own stock-market riches. Greed took hold.

Few seemed to care. The market was enchanted, part of an affluent and exciting time that seemed likely to continue forever. Politicians, professors, and businessmen proclaimed that this was a new era, where the old ups and downs no longer applied. Americans flourishing in the 1920s shared a feeling, said historian David M. Kennedy, "that they dwelt in a land and time of special promise."

Then came October 1929.

RIGHT: This famous January 1929 cartoon from *Forbes* magazine, titled "The Goal," illustrates the frenzy to get rich in the stock market. Ordinary people rush toward a ticker machine that printed out the latest stock prices.

WORD SPREAD QUICKLY on this crisp fall morning: Stocks were in big trouble. The boys selling the morning newspapers shouted the news. Serious-voiced announcers on the radio commented on it. On the street, everyone was talking about it. Something was terribly wrong with the stock market, the greatest fountain of wealth in the history of America.

In the financial district of New York City and in other offices where brokers sold stocks, people began to gather well before stock trading formally began at 10 A.M. Men and women, nervous and pale, rushed to grab seats in the special customers' rooms at brokerage houses all around Wall Street. One observer said they looked like "dying men counting their own last pulse beats."

People also hurried to the corner of Broad and Wall Streets, just across the way from the New York Stock Exchange. Hundreds, then thousands, filled the streets and sidewalks. Men in overcoats and fedoras and women on break from their stenographers' jobs crowded in front of J. P. Morgan & Company, the powerful banking company

These men and women packed the street and steps around a statue of George Washington because it was the best place to pick up any tidbits about what was happening inside the Exchange.

at 23 Wall Street. They lined the stairs of the Sub-treasury Building, right near the statue marking where George Washington was sworn in as the nation's first president. Usually, this kind of massive crowd gathered only for fires or to peer at the gore of some new crime. This day, though, there was nothing to see.

Fear and excitement had brought them, the kind of intense, heart-pounding emotion felt when something really bad is happening. If stocks were dropping, plans for the future were disappearing too. For some people gathered there, every cent they owned was riding on stocks, those odd pieces of paper that represented small stakes in American companies. For others, the stock market's climb had simply been an amazing thing to watch.

WHAT ARE STOCKS?

Businesses can raise money in lots of ways. They can go to a bank and borrow it. They can borrow money from investors that they will have to pay back later. Or they can share part of the company by selling stock, or shares of ownership.

The founders of a business start out owning their company. As their company grows, they may raise money from their friends or professional investors by selling more shares. When many investors own the shares, the business is considered a "public" company because the public has an ownership stake in it. At the top of public companies are boards of directors, whose job is to make sure the business's managers are working in the best interests of the many owners, or shareholders.

Investors buy a company's stock hoping the shares' value will increase as the business grows and improves. (After the purchase they get a stock certificate showing how many shares they own.) But buying stock is risky. Stock is never repaid like debt is. And if the business isn't successful, the stock's value can fall—or even become worthless.

Companies sell shares so they can expand their businesses or make them better, such as by building manufacturing plants, buying competitors, or developing new products. America's railroads, steel manufacturers, automobile makers, and telephone companies all were launched with the help of money from stock sales.

On Thursday, October 24, men and women left their jobs and homes to gather near the New York Stock Exchange as news of stock troubles spread.

In the 1920s many astonishing events had captivated the nation. Charles Lindbergh had successfully flown across the Atlantic, becoming a worldwide hero. Babe Ruth had blasted home runs in record numbers. Bobby Jones had dominated golf. Gangsters had shot and killed hundreds in Chicago. But the dramatic rise of the stock market outlasted and outroared them all. It had been a "magic carpet ride" that now seemed to be ending in a most spectacular way. As people gathered, they waited for details with a mixture of thrill and dread.

Motion-picture cameramen arrived to film the scene for the news-reels that ran in theaters before feature films. Hundreds of additional police, some on foot and some on horseback, were sent to keep the crowd moving. But this group was orderly; in fact, it was eerily somber, almost dazed by the mysterious events going on across the street.

For more than a year, the stock market had been the surest and easi-est way in the world to get rich. A ditty in *The Saturday Evening Post* captured the attitude:

"O hush thee, my babe, granny's bought some more shares,
Daddy's gone to play with the bulls and the bears,
Mother's buying on tips and she simply can't lose,
And baby shall have some expensive new shoes."

Companies had sold hundreds of thousands of shares to the public to raise money to build new plants or to expand their businesses. Once the companies sold them, those shares were traded between buyers and sellers in places like the New York Stock Exchange. People invested in these stocks hoping the companies would do well. Well-managed companies

WHAT IS A STOCK EXCHANGE?

People who want to buy or sell stocks need to have a central place to do it. A stock exchange is a marketplace where stocks can be bought and sold.

In the early days of the United States, a few formal and organized exchanges sprang up in many major cities to trade in securities, the broad name for debt and stock owned by investors. Many of the exchanges operated outdoors well into the nineteenth century. In New York City, traders stood under lampposts on the curbs along Broad and Wall streets, trading stocks like they were fruits and vegetables.

The bigger, more formal exchanges were open only to members, who traded stocks and debt on behalf of other investors in exchange for a fee, or commission. These exchanges pledged to run a "free and open" marketplace. That meant no single person or group dominated or controlled the trading. Trades were to be made in the open and out loud, and prices were posted for all to see. The hope was—and is—that trading information available to one group of people would be available to all investors.

In the 1920s two major markets operated in New York City: the New York Stock Exchange and the New York Curb Market, later called the American Stock Exchange. Nationwide there were more than twenty stock exchanges.

On October 24, newspapers rushed
out their afternoon editions with the
Stock Exchange news. With the ticker
running behind, investors were eager
to see the papers to find out what was
happening to their stocks.

DDAY LOWS.,.DOW: -33.53...ATT: -27...GM: -8.38...RADIO: -24...STEEL: -10.50... MIDDAY LOWS...DOW:

that make popular products usually see their sales and profits—and stock prices—grow. Sometimes, though, investors buy stocks for emotional reasons. They like the name, or the idea, or even an advertisement for a company. That kind of excitement can take on a life of its own, sending a stock soaring or crashing for no rational reason.

People who had bought a piece of General Electric, Montgomery Ward, or Westinghouse in March 1928 had witnessed a buying frenzy as those shares had at least doubled in value in eighteen short months. Which stocks were hot and who had been lucky had been trolley-car chitchat, party talk, and dinner-table conversation for months. Defying gravity and common sense, dozens of stocks had jumped from $20 or $30 to $200 or $300 a share. What was to keep them from going to $400 or higher?

Hardly anything seemed capable of slowing the climb. But on a brutally hot and humid day in early September 1929, prices had started slipping and sliding. Such "breaks" in the market weren't that unusual—in fact, stocks had dropped sharply the previous December and again in March. The smart players saw those declines as an opportunity. In the past few years, every fall had been followed by a recovery. Each time, stock prices climbed even higher than before.

At first, the shift that started in September seemed healthy, a natural cooling off of an overheated market. But in October there had been some ugly days when stock sales were too heavy. The market seemed less sure. Still, the problems didn't appear to be too serious.

Then, in the last hour of trading on Wednesday, October 23, stock prices seemed to melt. Out of nowhere, everyone seemed to want to sell at the same time. Some stocks dropped a shocking $5 or $15 a share in frantic trading because no one would step up to buy them. More than 2.6 million shares changed hands in the chaotic final hour of trading, as many as might trade in a regular day. When the gong that ended trading rang at 3 P.M., the market was weak and trembling.

On the morning of October 24, the virus seemed to have spread. People were selling shares at any price they could get, and prices were plunging with a violence never seen before. "In a society built largely on confidence, with real wealth expressed more or less inaccurately by pieces of paper, the entire fabric of economic stability threatened to come toppling down," the New York *World* reported somberly.

All over Wall Street, there were rumors. Half a dozen brokers working inside the Stock Exchange had collapsed and were taken to hospitals, it was whispered. Eleven well-known speculators had already killed themselves. Men, broken and broke, were jumping from buildings! The crowd craned their necks to look up at windows. Ambulances rushed to respond.

Small-time investors visited "customers' rooms" at their brokerage houses to get stock information. Clerks posted the latest prices as they came over the ticker tape. Clerks who were fast and accurate could earn generous tips.

One person spotted a man atop a high building looking down at them, and assumed the man was about to jump. The crowd bunched together to watch. But the man turned out to be making some repairs, and when he went back inside, the throng was disappointed. A London newspaper reported that so many distraught stock owners jumped from windows that bodies were littering the streets of Manhattan. Not so. In truth, there were no suicides on Wall Street that day, though many people may have felt as if their world were ending.

There was, though, an ominous feeling, a deep-in-the-gut sensation that something powerful and painful was unfolding. From across the street at the Stock Exchange came a weird and relentless roar that could be heard clearly by the crowd. Steady and high-pitched, it was the combined voices of more than a thousand men inside trying to hold on to the last shreds of the greatest financial boom ever. "It was the voice of the Street," said *The New York Times*, "now hopeful, now tragic, making audible the history of a momentous day in the market."

OCTOBER

24

Sell!

A New York *World* artist captured the pandemonium on the floor of the New York Stock Exchange on October 24. (Photographs weren't allowed during the trading day.) In the foreground is Post 2, where the stock of U.S. Steel was traded.

THE PEOPLE CROWDING into the streets outside the New York Stock Exchange could only imagine the insanity around Michael J. Meehan. Standing at his usual spot at Post 12 on the Stock Exchange trading floor, he couldn't work fast enough this morning to keep up. In a decade of stock trading, he had never seen anything quite like this. Screaming, pushing traders and flying paper surrounded him. All around him, people wanted to sell, and they all wanted to sell right then. But he needed buyers to make the trades, and they were nowhere to be found.

On this wild Thursday in late October, Mr. Meehan had been in constant motion even before the market opened. Worried about the torrent of stock sales late Wednesday afternoon, he knew stock owners were getting fidgety. Orders had poured in all morning to the hundreds of telephone operators who lined the sides of the huge trading floor. They came from brokerage offices around the country. The phone operators would summon individual brokers by posting their special numbers on huge boards on two sides of the trading floor. The brokers were to rush to the phone booths to pick up their instructions. The orders were coming in so furiously that the black annunciator boards buzzed and rattled as numbers were displayed.

When the gong rang at 10 A.M., the market opened, in the words of one old-timer, "like a bolt out of hell." Though hundreds of brokers were working, they couldn't get to all the orders fast enough. Within minutes, prices started to sink, weighed down by a powerful, unseen force. By 11 A.M., a thick group struggled to get Mike Meehan's attention at Post 12. Red-faced men hollered and waved fistfuls of paper orders at Post 4, trying to sell General Motors.

Post 2, where U.S. Steel was traded, was "the center of a sort of madness" as masses of traders waved and gestured to be heard. The stock had closed the day before at $205, and some staunch supporters were buying, trying to keep the price of this well-known company above $200. But the buyers couldn't offset the surge of orders to *Sell! Sell! Sell!* The price careened to $194. From the mob, a voice could be heard "bellowing like a lunatic."

The price declines were eye-popping. General Electric's price slid $25 a share, Westinghouse was down $20, General Motors fell more than $12. The shares of Auburn Auto, another car maker, had dropped $77 a share on Wednesday. On Thursday, it plunged another $70, to $190. Millions of shares were changing hands as small and large investors tried to preserve something of their winnings and get out. With each drop in price, someone was losing money.

Mike Meehan struggled to keep his post under control. A short and energetic red-haired man with metal-rimmed glasses, Mr. Meehan had one of the most famous names on the New York Stock Exchange

THE OPENING GONG

The New York Stock Exchange has opened and closed each trading day with the ringing of a bell since it started continuous trading in the 1870s. No trading is to take place before the day's opening bell or after its closing bell.

The first bell was a Chinese gong. But, in the early 1900s, the Exchange moved to a new building and began using a brass bell. At eighteen inches in diameter, the New York Stock Exchange bell is larger and louder than most bells made today.

floor. His firm, M. J. Meehan & Company, bought and sold stocks for others for a commission, or fee. But he was also the specialist, the key trader, in the stock of Radio Corporation of America, perhaps the most glamorous stock of the day.

Radios didn't even exist in the United States until the fall of 1920. But within a few years of their introduction, everyone wanted one of those wireless wonders to follow baseball games, hear politicians, and listen to popular crooners like Rudy Vallee and shows like *Amos 'n' Andy*. Before long, one out of every three American homes had radios.

Radio Corporation made a lot of radios, but it also did much more. It was helping movies talk, it sent wireless messages, and it had recently purchased the Victor Talking Machine Company, a major maker of early record players. It was working with General Motors to make the first radios for automobiles. Its National Broadcasting Company, also known as NBC, owned twenty-five radio stations from coast to coast.

As Radio's specialist at the Stock Exchange, Mr. Meehan bought or sold Radio shares, but he didn't do it for himself. He did it so there would be a market for the shares, a place for others to go to buy and

The New York Stock Exchange floor looked tame when empty, but on a busy day, it was crammed with traders and brokers hurrying from trading post to trading post. Brokerage firms could send messages to their brokers by posting numbers on the black annunciator board on the left. Visitors watched from the balcony on the far side.

sell Radio shares. Stocks were traded on the Stock Exchange trading floor, but only the 1,375 members of the New York Stock Exchange could do business there. Members were traders, who bought and sold stocks for themselves, or brokers, who bought and sold for their customers. If someone wanted to buy or sell Radio's shares, he called a broker, who called a New York Stock Exchange member. That member would come to Mike Meehan at Post 12, and Mr. Meehan would try to find the right price to satisfy everyone.

Mr. Meehan, thirty-eight years old, had come to America with his Irish parents in 1902. As a young man with little education, he knew nothing of high finance. But he was a natural salesman and very ambitious. When a cigar store hired him, he hustled up more business by taking cigars to theater

Michael J. Meehan was one of the most famous stock market figures of the 1920s. The flower in his buttonhole was a trademark of successful financiers.

doors and selling them as patrons left the shows. From there, he became the manager of a downtown ticket agency, selling Broadway tickets to Wall Street clients. He knew how to land good seats, and his best clients rewarded him with stock tips. He was making $5,000 a year, a nice wage. But his customers told him that he easily could do better in the stock market.

Confident he could do it, Mike told his wife, Elizabeth, that he had an opportunity to make more money. He warned that taking it would mean giving up a regular weekly paycheck. With three children already and another on the way, Elizabeth wasn't sure this was a good idea, but she gave her okay. "If I'd ever said no, I'd have always been wondering 'what if,'" she would tell her grandson Terence S. Meehan. Besides, she added, "I was well-schooled and educated in how to scrape by."

After some rough months Mr. Meehan built a roaring business on the New York Curb Exchange, a wilder stock exchange that once operated outdoors on a sidewalk. Within two years he had enough to buy a seat on the prestigious New York Stock Exchange for $90,000. A few years later, when Radio Corporation of America's stock was listed on the New York Stock Exchange, Mr. Meehan became its biggest fan. He told everyone, from elevator boys to executives, to buy it.

Mr. Meehan believed in the future of radio and the idea of someday transmitting pictures in a newfangled technology called television. He also believed in his own sales skills. Radio never paid its shareholders a dividend—a payment from profits that was considered a sure sign of a sound investment. But Mr. Meehan knew that if he could get the right people interested, Radio's stock would take off.

With his ties to Radio, Mike Meehan became one of the biggest players at the New York Stock Exchange. He had eight memberships, or "seats," more than any other firm. M. J. Meehan & Company had nine branch offices and a staff of four hundred. But he considered himself one of the guys and didn't want to be anything else. He wasn't a fancy dresser and didn't worry much about appearances, except to avoid the color green. His brother once had dared him to wear a green tie on the floor of the Stock Exchange. Mr. Meehan lost so much money with the tie on that he burned the tie and swore off green forever. "The map of Ireland's all over my face," he said. "What do I need with a green tie?"

In Mr. Meehan's early days on the Stock Exchange, the trading floor was relatively calm—almost boring. Men in gray suits, many sporting a fresh flower in their buttonholes, wandered about, talking in numbers. On a normal day, about half the brokers and traders on the floor appeared to be doing nothing more than hanging around, swapping jokes. The rest gathered in groups around trading posts, calling

WHAT IS THE NEW YORK STOCK EXCHANGE?

The New York Stock Exchange is the country's oldest and most prestigious marketplace for trading stocks and bonds.

Located at the corner of Broad Street and Wall Street in New York City's financial district, the Exchange and its noisy trading floor are considered the heart of Wall Street, where billions of dollars of investments change hands every day.

The Stock Exchange dates its start to 1792, when twenty-four prominent merchants and brokers gathered under a buttonwood tree on Wall Street and agreed to trade with one another. Before that, government bonds and other securities had been traded haphazardly at periodic meetings. The men who started the Exchange wanted a marketplace that would be fair, responsible, and trustworthy.

For many years no women were allowed on the Stock Exchange floor, even as clerks. The first woman to work on the trading floor was a telephone operator, hired in the 1940s.

To have their shares listed on the Exchange, companies must meet certain requirements intended to ensure that they are reputable and will treat shareholders fairly.

Only members of the New York Stock Exchange can trade stocks there. Members must buy one of the limited "seats" on the Exchange, so named because until the 1870s, members actually had assigned chairs on the trading floor. The Exchange was once known as the New York Stock and Exchange Board, but over time, the name was shortened. Still, the Exchange is often called "the Big Board," reflecting its old name and its role as the most established securities marketplace.

23

out prices as specialists like Mr. Meehan accepted bids and wrote them down in ledger books.

In the past year, though, the volume of stock trading grew so fast that the systems were pushed to their limits. The Stock Exchange replaced tall posts that looked like large streetlights with massive, U-shaped booths. At Post 12, a sign showed that Radio Corporation's stock was traded there. Dials displayed the last sales price. Inside the "U," clerks kept track of paperwork. On the outside of the "U," a paunchy Michael Meehan held court, his red hair combed back from his forehead.

New trading posts installed in 1929 were shaped like horseshoes. The latest stock prices were posted at the top. Specialists like Michael J. Meehan stood outside making trades. Clerks worked inside the horseshoe, handling paperwork.

In 1928 and 1929 the Stock Exchange grew busier and busier as an increasing number of Americans came to believe the stock market was a good place for their money to grow. Some observers said that Mike Meehan single-handedly drew them in.

In March 1928 the price of Radio's stock had suddenly zoomed to incredible heights. Within weeks, Radio became the stock of the "in" generation. Mr. Meehan, a once-anonymous stock trader, emerged as something of a Wall Street legend.

The quick rise in Radio stock price appeared to have happened almost overnight, but it actually reflected weeks of backroom planning by a small group of wealthy and prominent businessmen. New York Stock Exchange officials bragged that their exchange was a free and fair marketplace where stocks sold for what buyers were willing to pay and sellers were willing to accept. But that was only partly true. Some powerful men, like William C. Durant, the founder of General Motors, knew ways to make stock prices dance. These "bulls," people who believed that stock prices were going to go up, thought that General Motors and Radio Corporation were *the* stocks to buy.

As a group, Mr. Durant and his powerful friends began buying shares of General Motors and Radio Corporation in early March 1928. On the New York Stock Exchange floor, Mike Meehan made sure their buying got plenty of attention. The Stock Exchange's ticker, a service that sent out prices to nearly ten thousand ticker-tape machines in New York and distant cities like San Francisco, Dallas, Atlanta, and Denver, reported each trade and the steady climb in price. To experienced stock-market players, a story emerged from the endless stream of numbers on the narrow ticker

A clerk types the latest stock prices into a ticker machine. The prices usually printed out quickly on ticker tape across the country. But during the crash, so many prices changed so quickly, that the ticker tape ran hours behind.

INEXPERIENCED SNAKE-CHARMERS BEWARE

STOCK MARKET

Despite frequent cartoon warnings like this one, few seemed to heed the message.

tape: Smart people must like this stock. And smart people buy only when they think a stock is going up.

People who didn't know about the plans of Mr. Durant's group began to buy General Motors and Radio shares too. With so many people trying to buy the stock, Radio's stock price made a stunning jump, climbing more than $20 in just two days, to $120.50 a share. Newspapers noticed the sudden and unusual rise, and the heavy trading that went with it. Stories about Radio Corporation and its soaring shares moved from the financial pages, tucked behind the sports scores, to the front page. RADIO RISES TO LEAD IN BIGGEST MARKET, *The New York Times* announced.

Some Stock Exchange specialists might have wanted to take it slow and trade only a few shares at a time, trying to keep the price stable. But Mike Meehan liked to swing for the fences, "to take a big position in everything," said his grandson Michael Nesbit. The next week trading was heavy in Radio again, with as much as $1 million in stock changing hands at a time. So many orders were coming in that brokers descended on Mr. Meehan and Post 12 to buy Radio Stock. The

Sports teams have offensive and defensive players. Stock markets have bulls and bears. Bulls believe stocks are going up. They buy stocks and hold them. If the stock does go up in price, bulls can sell their stock for more than they paid. When the stock market is going up, investors call it a "bull market."

Bears, by contrast, believe stocks will go down. People who think stocks will go down don't want to own those stocks. To make their bets, they "sell short." That is, a bearish investor borrows stock from a broker and sells it, promising to pay the stock back later. If the stock falls in price, the bear buys the stock back at the cheaper price and pays back the broker at the lower price. His profit is the difference between the price he received when he sold the stock and the price he paid when he bought it back. When stocks overall are falling sharply, investors call it a "bear market."

Where the names came from isn't really known. One theory is that bears use their paws to bring down their prey, while bulls are known for ducking their heads and sending enemies skyward. Bears, sometimes called "short-sellers," also may have gotten their nickname from an old saying, "He sold the bearskin before he caught the bear," since they hope to make money on something they don't actually own.

Being a bear is riskier than being a bull. For example, a bullish investor could buy 100 shares of stock for $10 a share, paying $1,000. If the stock goes to $20 a share, the bull has doubled his money. If the stock keeps going up, he can make an unlimited amount of profit. But the most he can lose is his initial $1,000.

A bearish investor could borrow those 100 shares and sell them for $10 each. If the stock slides to $5, he makes $500. The most profit he can make is $1,000—if the stock goes to zero. But what if the stock soars to $40 a share? Ouch! He has to pay $4,000 to "cover" his position and repay the broker. Bears can lose an unlimited amount of money.

yelling-and-pushing throng tore the collar of his shirt and nearly pulled his coat off his back. In the frenzied last half hour of trading on Monday, March 12, 1928, visitors to the Stock Exchange "got the impression that they were watching a street fight with policemen in the center vainly trying to take control of the situation." Clothes disheveled, Mr. Meehan left the floor looking like a soldier returning from battle.

To the casual observer, the leap in Radio's stock price looked like demand for the stock had gone wild. But behind the scenes was a classic stock-market fight. Big "bulls," Wall Street's optimists, were beating up on "bears," Wall Street's pessimists. The more the bulls bought and touted Radio's shares, the harder it was for the bears to bet that the shares would go down. As the stock skyrocketed, the bulls were making fistfuls of money, and the bears were taking losses by the bucketful.

With Radio now trading at $146 a share, up about $50 in eight days, Mr. Meehan was hailed for his stock-trading daring and bravado. *The New York Times* gushed, "he has made and unmade millionaires within less than a single week, and he has staged one of the most dramatic moves in any one story in the history of the Exchange...."

The moves inside the New York Stock Exchange were extraordinary. But what was happening outside the Exchange was just as amazing—and more significant. Everywhere brokerage firms were seeing a rush of new customers. A "flame of speculative excitement ... appears to be sweeping the country from coast to coast," *The New York Times* said, and it was pushing trading volume to new records almost daily. Suddenly, big, rich investors found themselves next to drivers and teachers who were trying to buy stocks. Brokerage houses opened special rooms for women, where they could sip tea and watch stock prices. Customers' rooms were filled with amateur investors watching intently as young clerks posted stock prices on chalkboards or as the ticker passed overhead on a lighted screen.

As the stock market soared, cartoonists made fun of—and warned about—the growing fascination with stocks.

Comedian Groucho Marx of the famous Marx Brothers was often one of those new, small-stock players, regularly visiting his broker's office in Long Island, New York, to check on his investments. His purchases, the entertainer thought, were a "sound, money-making venture," a partnership with America's best businesses. "What an easy racket," he'd exclaim with excitement when he would return from the broker's. Radio "went up seven points since this morning. I just made myself $7,000."

Tales of manicurists and elevator boys making half a million dollars were common—even if they probably weren't true. Everyone seemed to have a stock tip, the office boy, the grocer, the lady next door. One big Wall Street trader reported that his chauffeur had informed him that Radio's stock was going up. How did the chauffeur know? He had heard it "down at the garage."

In late March 1928, Radio took off again in gold-rush fashion for no apparent reason. The New York Stock Exchange's total trading volume reached nearly 5 million shares, the kind of activity Wall Street veterans had only dreamed of. Then, on March 30, 1928, Mike Meehan and his friends capped off their feat with fireworks: In one day Radio's stock rocketed $24.50 a share to close at $195—higher even than the stock of giant General Motors. Radio's price had doubled in less than a month, and its ascent had been simply stunning.

On that March day a speculator stood at the ticker machine at a busy brokerage firm, entranced by the ever-rising price of Radio shares. Dollar signs seemed to prance on the tape in front of his eyes as he imagined one stock after another doing the same thing. He couldn't control his excitement. "Everything is going to $500!" he exclaimed.

The public had been smitten. The greatest bull market of all time was underway.

In 1928 the Dow Jones Industrial Average climbed 48 percent in one of the biggest annual gains in history. It had taken more than

The Dow Jones Industrial Average is the oldest and most famous indicator of the stock market. When people ask how the stock market did on any given day, they usually are asking whether the Dow Jones Industrial Average went up or down.

Charles Henry Dow created the index in 1896, choosing twelve well-known, large, and reputable industrial companies, averaging their stock prices, and dividing by twelve. The average, sometimes called simply the "Dow," is intended to show generally the trend of the broader stock market.

The average was expanded to twenty stocks in 1916 and to thirty in 1928, just as the stock market really was taking off. Among the new companies added in the 1928 expansion were established players like Chrysler Corporation, Bethlehem Steel Corporation, and the cutting edge Radio Corporation of America. Although it is still called an average, the Dow is no longer calculated by adding up the stock prices and dividing by thirty. The divisor decreased over the years as companies paid special dividends or issued more shares.

The editors of *The Wall Street Journal*, owned by Dow Jones and Company, oversee the index and change the stocks in the Dow when companies are acquired, go bankrupt, or change their business. The following companies were part of the Dow Jones Industrial Average in October 1929:

1. Allied Chemical & Dye Corp.
2. American Can Co.
3. American Smelting & Refining
4. American Sugar Refining Co.
5. American Tobacco
6. Atlantic Refining Co.
7. B. F. Goodrich Co.
8. Bethlehem Steel Corp.
9. Chrysler Corp.
10. Curtiss-Wright Corp.
11. F. W. Woolworth Co.
12. General Electric Co.
13. General Foods Corp.
14. General Motors Corp.
15. General Railway Signal Corp.
16. International Harvester Co.
17. International Nickel Co.
18. Mack Trucks Inc.
19. Nash Motors Co.
20. National Cash Register Co.
21. North American Co.
22. Paramount Famous Lasky Corp.
23. Radio Corporation of America
24. Sears, Roebuck & Co.
25. Standard Oil Co. (New Jersey)
26. Texas Co.
27. Texas Gulf Sulphur
28. U.S. Steel Corp.
29. Union Carbide & Carbon Corp.
30. Westinghouse Electric & Manufacturing Co.

twenty years, from 1906 to 1927, for this key stock-market indicator to climb to 200 from 100. But in just over a year, the average jumped from 200 to 300, reaching its new high on the last day of 1928.

Mike Meehan, having helped kindle the boom, wanted to keep the excitement alive. Knowing that the wealthy often sailed to Europe for vacations, he won Stock Exchange approval to put M. J. Meehan brokerage offices on three luxury ships. Equipped with radios to receive stock prices during the trading day and special equipment for sending private messages, these offices opened in August 1929 to a flurry of publicity. Some commentators saw the offices as a sign of modern, technological progress. Others fretted that ocean voyages would lose "their greatest charm, which was to get entirely out of reach of the office." But the ship brokerages were a hit with first-class passengers. Their customer rooms, each complete with twenty fat leather easy chairs, were often full of speculators checking on their stocks. In late October 1929 the *SS Berengaria* set sail from Europe to New York with several millionaires onboard.

On October 24, the impact of what was happening on the New York Stock Exchange was reverberating over land and sea. In London, where the market had closed for the day, brokers set up shop on the street and traded American shares under a pouring rain. Investors hurried to their brokers' offices in Detroit, Boston, Philadelphia, and other cities. Shares were falling on regional exchanges in Baltimore, Chicago, and San Francisco.

The customers' room on the *Berengaria*, in the middle of the ocean, was stuffed with concerned stock-market players. Card games, letter writing, and champagne breakfasts had ended abruptly when passengers heard that the market was falling. As one sinking stock price after another was posted, a chorus rose in the Meehan broker's office that was echoed in customers' rooms everywhere: "Sell now! Sell now!"

One woman on the *Berengaria* lost $160,000 during the morning.

Helena Rubinstein, a clever and tough cosmetics maker who was going to New York to promote her makeup line, had settled into a front-row seat. She watched, silent and expressionless, from her leather armchair as her Westinghouse stock dropped from $190 to $173. Finally she raised a hand and gave an order to sell 50,000 shares, more than $8 million in stock. In the minutes it took to make the trade, the price fell to $168. In

PRICES, THEN AND NOW

Prices change all the time. Sometimes strong demand for a product will push the price up. Other times, improvements in technology or the manufacturing process will bring prices down.

A rise in the general cost of living is called inflation. Between 1929 and 2001 the cost of living generally went up. As a result, $1 in 1929 purchased about the same as $10.36 in 2001.

Of course, the prices of different goods climbed by different amounts. Cars and homes cost much more today because modern automobiles and houses are bigger and have many more features than they had in 1929. Other goods are relatively cheap. Here are a few examples:

Average individual income
  In 1929: $6,132
  In 1999: $46,078

Average new single-family home
  In 1929: $4,915
  In 2001: $211,900

Typical car
  In 1929: Ford Fordor, 2-window
    sedan: $625
  In 2001: Ford Taurus: $21,000

Sirloin steak, 1 lb.
  In 1929: 52 cents
  In 2001: $4.45

Whole milk, 1 gallon
  In 1929: 58 cents
  In 2001: $2.88

Bananas, 1 lb.
  In 1929: 10 cents
  In 2001: 51 cents

Potatoes, 1 lb.
  In 1929: 3 cents
  In 2001: 39 cents

Sugar, 1 lb.
  In 1929: 6 cents
  In 2001: 43 cents

just two hours she had watched $1 million of her fortune evaporate. In today's dollars that would be like losing more than $10 million!

While his broker's offices on the sea were swamped with orders, Mr. Meehan was facing more serious troubles on the Stock Exchange floor. He couldn't find any buyers. He was dropping prices by $1, then $2, then $5, and sometimes $10 before someone would buy the shares. Having helped invite so many people to this stock-market party, Mr. Meehan could only watch as the affair got out of hand.

Other traders "raised their faces, rich with expensive Florida tan, and called and called again for buyers who did not come," reported the New York *World*. "They dangled slips of paper under each other's noses like anglers tempting trout." But there were no takers.

Rules of the Stock Exchange specifically said that members on the floor should not run, curse, or push, but in the hysterical frenzy of midday trading, men

WE were crowded in the cabin
  Watching figures on the Board;
It was midnight on the ocean
  And a tempest loudly roared.

We were watching the quotations
  With a certain sad appeal;
Some were short in General Motors,
  Some were long on U. S. Steel.

And, as timidly a tourist
  Took a chance on twenty shares—
"We are lost!" the Captain shouted,
  As he staggered down the stairs.

"I've got a tip," he faltered,
  "Straight by wireless from the aunt
Of a fellow who's related
  To a cousin of Durant."

At these awful words we shuddered
  And the stoutest bull grew sick,
While the brokers cried "More margin!"
  And the ticker ceased to tick.

But the Captain's little daughter
  Said, "I do not understand—
Isn't Morgan on the ocean
  Just the same as on the land?"

—From the Spokane *Spokesman-Review*.

M. J. Meehan's on-ship brokerage was such a phenomenon that many articles were written about it—and at least one poem.

were doing all three. Only those on the floor knew how truly bad the carnage was. Clerks were punching in the latest stock prices into the ticker machine as fast as they could. On a normal day the prices would show up on ticker-tape machines shortly after the numbers were keyed in. But with so much activity, the ticker machines, printing only 285 characters a minute, simply could not keep up.

By midday the prices clacking out were nearly two hours old. Brokerage houses, thinking certain stocks were down a horrifying $5 or $10 a share, phoned the Stock Exchange's quotation service to get the latest prices. They were shocked to hear from telephone operators that the declines were actually much worse. Without reliable information about what was happening, people grew frantic. How much were they losing? How much more could they afford to lose? Without any answers, some hurried to dump their shares before it was too late. More and more sell orders cascaded in.

It was a panic, said Richard Whitney, vice president of the New York Stock Exchange, where "all at once, the inconceivable terrors of the unknown and the unfamiliar are thrust upon the public mind; confidence is paralyzed, and until it is restored, chaos reigns."

Nothing, it seemed, could stop the slide.

OCTOBER

24

WHITE KNIGHTS
TO THE RESCUE

By a strange coincidence, Winston Churchill, Great Britain's former Chancellor of the Exchequer, happened to be in New York for a visit on October 24, 1929. After an early lunch, he found himself in the crowded visitors' gallery of the New York Stock Exchange. A stock speculator himself, the future prime minister of Great Britain watched the noisy and hectic scene with interest. But while others saw craziness, he saw something else.

"I expected to see pandemonium; but the spectacle that met my eyes was one of surprising calm and orderliness," he wrote. Exchange members were "walking to and fro like a slow-motion picture of a disturbed antheap, offering each other enormous blocks of securities at a third of their old prices and half their present value, and for many minutes together finding no one strong enough to pick up the sure fortunes they were compelled to offer."

Mr. Churchill moved on shortly after, and Stock Exchange officials, worried about what *they* saw on the floor, decided to close the visitors' gallery. More than seven hundred people already had signed the guest register, a record for any day.

Outside, the gallery-closing turned into rumors that the Stock Exchange was shutting its doors to keep the disaster from growing worse. Fear again rose up in the huge crowd at the corner of Broad and Wall Streets. Once, in the 1600s, a large wooden wall had lined this street, built by the Dutch to protect them from enemies. The wall had been gone some three hundred years, and the people on Wall Street today felt strangely vulnerable.

Some, though, had their hopes up. Just a few minutes before, a man in shirtsleeves was seen making his way to the Corner, the streets where the Stock Exchange and J. P. Morgan and Company offices met. Some in the crowd recognized the man as Charles E. Mitchell, chairman of National City Bank, the nation's largest bank. Thomas W. Lamont, the affable Morgan partner, had called a meeting.

Thomas W. Lamont was a senior partner at J. P. Morgan and a highly regarded financial adviser.

John Pierpont "Jack" Morgan, Jr., senior partner of the powerful Morgan bank his father founded, was out of the country. Mr. Lamont, a clever and admired financier, was in charge. A friendly man with a strong intellectual bent, Mr. Lamont had started his career as a newspaper reporter before developing a talent for fixing troubled companies. From there, he moved to banking and became a partner in the revered Morgan firm in 1911. Now fifty-nine years old, he had advised the president and Congress and Cabinet members on sensitive financial issues and helped several foreign countries with debt matters.

He also had played a role in creating today's market. During the World War, he hit the road to encourage citizens to buy Liberty Bonds to pay for the war effort. In numerous speeches and articles, he encouraged patriots to consider how much they could save over the next several months. Then, he told them, they could buy a generous Liberty Bond by putting a little money down and borrowing the rest from a bank. By scrimping, they could pay

39

WHAT ARE BONDS?

One way for a government or company to borrow money for a long period of time is to borrow money from the public by selling bonds. In exchange for using an investor's money, the government or company makes a regular cash or "interest" payment to the bondholder. At some point the bond comes due, and the company or government repays the debt.

The United States government first sold bonds to finance the Revolutionary War. It has sold debt to finance every war since then, as well as to raise money for many other things. States, cities, and school districts sell bonds to build roads, libraries, and schools.

Debts that have to be repaid in five years or fewer are often called "notes." Bonds may not have to be repaid for ten, thirty, or even fifty years.

The price of a bond can change. But bond prices are much less volatile than stock prices. They go up or down based on interest rates. Companies that take on too much debt can get in trouble when their business isn't strong enough to allow them to repay their borrowings. But government bonds are considered to be among the safest investments around because governments can raise taxes to repay their debts.

their own loan back over six months. The bond—essentially a loan to the government—would pay holders 4 percent interest a year for the privilege of using their money. The government, in time, would pay the money back.

"The thing I want to impress on you is the necessity of looking forward, of being bold and of subscribing to the loan *every cent* that you can save from your income in the next six months," Mr. Lamont lectured. "You mustn't be timid. Think of the courage that our soldiers must show in the trenches, and then stop for a moment and consider whether you are showing anything like equal courage in the way you are proposing to handle this loan."

People listened, and over two years, the Liberty Loan program raised $18.5 billion from bond sales to ordinary people. From these simple government bonds sold during war, Americans learned about investing in stocks and bonds. They also learned how to borrow money for an investment that might bring them money in the future.

The U.S. government sold Liberty Bonds for as little as $10 to raise money for the first World War. An investor could buy a bond that the government would eventually repay.

In fact, some might say they learned that lesson too well. Putting some money down to buy stock and borrowing the rest became increasingly popular as the stock market boomed. Many thought that the buy-now, pay-later practice, which grew from seeds planted by the Liberty Bond sales, was one reason that stocks were in a free fall at this very moment.

To see what, if anything, might be done about the calamity at the Stock Exchange across the street, Mr. Lamont had summoned the city's top bankers to a lunch-hour meeting. Because phone lines were jammed, it had taken ten minutes just to reach Mr. Mitchell two blocks away at National City Bank. Albert H. Wiggin, chairman of Chase National Bank, watching the devastation coming across his ticker, proclaimed, "This is no bear market, it's a panic—and we have got to do something." Answering Mr. Lamont's call, he put on his hat and headed for the Corner. Joining Mr. Mitchell and Mr. Wiggin around Mr. Lamont's rolltop desk were top officers of two other prestigious banks, Guaranty Trust Company and Bankers Trust Company, as well as George Whitney, a Morgan partner and the brother of Richard Whitney, the Stock Exchange vice president.

The meeting lasted just twenty minutes. But in that short time the bankers drew up a list of endangered stocks and each agreed to contribute millions of dollars to buy shares in those companies to restore confidence in the market. (How much they actually put up isn't

To encourage purchases, the New York Stock Exchange sponsored Liberty Bond rallies, like this one in 1917, when it turned the annunciator board into a giant billboard. Liberty Bonds gave many Americans their first taste of investing.

known. Newspapers noted that these banks had billions of dollars in resources, implying that they were willing to put up bundles. Most likely, each bank agreed to spend up to $20 million to bolster the market, or more than $100 million in all—a lot of money, though not as much as some believed.) The men left as quickly as they came, marching out of 23 Wall Street with grave faces into a crush of waiting newspaper reporters.

While the bankers returned to their offices, Mr. Lamont invited reporters to a short, impromptu press conference around his desk in the partners' area. The questions flew at him, but he was cautious in answering them. Silver-haired and aristocratic-looking, he was serious, but tried to sound reassuring. Mr. Lamont was, said reporter Claud Cockburn, like a "man who comes on the stage of a burning theater and urges everyone to keep perfectly cool, stating there is no cause for alarm." Mr. Lamont gestured with his eyepiece and spoke softly.

"There seems to be some distress selling on the Stock Exchange," he said with remarkable understatement, "and we had a meeting of the heads of several financial institutions to discuss the situation." Broker-age houses were weathering the storm just fine, he reassured the group. The bankers thought the problem was technical—that is, a stock-market problem—rather than a fundamental problem with business or the economy.

Would he predict what would happen to the market next? That wouldn't be prudent, he answered, but the bankers did believe the situation was "susceptible of betterment."

As the group broke up, the crowd at the Corner grew hopeful. Many remembered that back in 1907, J. Pierpont Morgan, Sr., had stepped in single-handedly to stop a banking and stock-market panic. Maybe the House of Morgan would come to the rescue again.

In customers' rooms, where investors were shell-shocked by what was happening at the Stock Exchange, people weren't sure what to think. At the Brooklyn brokerage firm of Boody and McLellan, a woman let out a shriek when the report of Mr. Lamont's comments— "There seems to be some distress selling"—came over the news tickers and flashed onto a screen. "Seems to be?" asked the woman, with a shrill, almost hysterical, cackle. For the first time that day, the room exploded in laughter, but only for a moment.

Inside the Exchange, there was actually a lull in the action after word of the Morgan meeting spread. Then, at 1:30 P.M., Richard Whitney appeared on the floor. Over six feet tall and with a haughty manner, he was the Stock Exchange's senior officer that day, for the exchange

Richard Whitney, the vice president of the New York Stock Exchange, was in charge when the stock market took a turn for the worse.

president was off on his honeymoon. But Mr. Whitney, who ran a small brokerage firm, also was considered J. P. Morgan's representative on the Stock Exchange floor, a position he had largely because his brother George was a Morgan partner.

Purposefully and confidently, he strode to Post 2, where the closely followed stock U.S. Steel was traded. The last sale had been at $205 a share. Now the price was down near $190, and there still weren't any buyers. In a loud, clear voice, almost shouting, Mr. Whitney called out a stunning order: 25,000 shares of Steel for $205 each. The mob around the post grew quiet. That was an enormous offer, some $5 million of stock! Then a cheer broke out. The Morgan-led banking group was supporting the market!

People on the New York Stock Exchange floor and in some brokerage houses could watch the latest stock prices projected on a screen. This photo, taken when the ticker enlarging machine was new, shows the old trading posts, shaped much like giant street lamps.

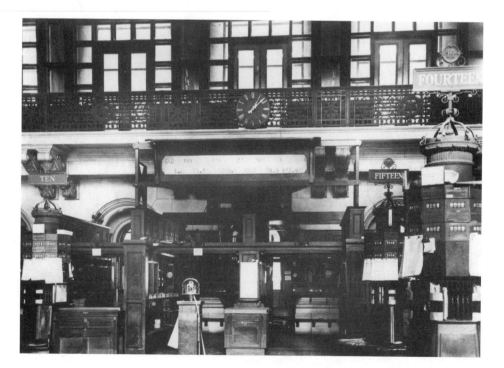

Mr. Whitney then moved around the floor, placing millions of dollars of orders for other shares. His actions electrified traders. Almost immediately, the mood changed. People slowly began to buy again. For the rest of the day, trading was furious. Steel's shares, which had been down more than $10, actually ended the day up about $2. Auburn Auto spiked up $43. Radio and General Electric bounced up, though both ended the day lower than they started.

When the gong rang at 3 P.M., the calls and yells of traders and floor brokers turned into a collective howl, a combination of groans, boos, and moans of relief. Exhausted and dripping with sweat, some traders leaned against the posts. Men stood dazed, holding handfuls of unfinished orders. Overwhelmed clerks threw torn paper, ticker tape, and memo pads in the air until it looked like a parade had come by.

In brokerage houses and in cities across the country, hours more would pass before the full extent of the smash-up and partial recovery was clear. The ticker was so tremendously behind and trading had been so enormously heavy that the glass-topped machine didn't finish tapping out the last of the day's prices until just after 7:08 P.M., more than four hours after the market closed. The final tally was dreadful. Nearly 13 million shares had been traded. Stock prices had fallen an estimated $3 billion.

In Washington, the Federal Reserve, the nation's central bank, met twice during the day. The concerns were so great that Treasury Secretary Andrew Mellon sat in on the afternoon meeting. But the central bank decided to wait and watch rather than take any action.

Colonel John W. Prentiss of the brokerage firm Hornblower & Weeks called about thirty other firms that sold stocks to the public to a meeting. The group agreed to show an optimistic face, hoping to calm customers and keep them from selling hysterically. In a daily market letter written to advise customers, Hornblower & Weeks said the day's selling was excessive. It believed that on Friday, the market "should start laying the foundation for the constructive advance which we believe will characterize 1930." The firm also bought advertisements in eighty-five newspapers, stating, "We believe that present conditions are favorable for advantageous investment in standard American securities."

Business leaders from San Francisco to Chicago to Wilmington hurried to declare that the storm had been vicious but had now passed. Stock prices were no longer inflated, and industry remained in good shape.

"This crash is not going to have much effect upon business," said Arthur Reynolds, chairman of Continental Illinois Bank.

"I see nothing to worry about," insisted Mr. Mitchell, the National City chairman who had helped prop up the market.

"Prices were literally slaughtered," *The Wall Street Journal* reported. But, "at the close, 90 percent of the Street believed that the worst was over and that stocks would not return to their low levels."

Brokerage firms and the Stock Exchange were swamped with paperwork. Trades had to be handwritten in ledger books, and money and stock certificates had to be collected and transferred. Accounts had to be reviewed. Hotels ran out of rooms, and restaurants were packed with people working into the night to get the accounting books in order so the markets could open the

We believe that present conditions are favorable for advantageous investment in standard American securities.

HORNBLOWER & WEEKS
ESTABLISHED 1888
42 Broadway   731 Fifth Avenue
NEW YORK CITY
BOSTON   NEW YORK   CHICAGO   CLEVELAND
DETROIT   PROVIDENCE   PORTLAND, ME.   PITTSBURGH
Members of the New York, Boston, Chicago, Cleveland, Pittsburgh and Detroit
Stock Exchanges and the New York Curb Exchange

Hornblower and Weeks ran this optimistic advertisement in eighty-five newspapers following the October 24 stock plunge.

So many shares changed hands on October 24 that men had to carry trunks filled with millions of dollars in stocks, trading records, and other paperwork from brokerage house to brokerage house in order to settle trades.

next day. A record-breaking number of telegrams were sent through Western Union Telegraph Company "from all corners of the earth." Messengers worked through the night to handle and deliver all the cables.

Another bunch was working late too. Mr. Lamont and the bankers group met in the afternoon. They decided to focus on supporting just a couple of dozen stocks, with Morgan partners managing the purchases.

After dinner, a bigger group of bankers met into the early hours of the morning. Some leaders feared that the stock decline could tumble into a full-fledged financial collapse. They wanted to close the New York Stock Exchange until the hysteria quieted down. But others argued that closing the Stock Exchange would only make investors more jittery.

The idea of closing was put aside. But the financial men, knowing how shaky the situation was, worried about what might still be ahead.

-6.38...ATT: -3...GM: -3.88...RADIO: -10.25...STEEL: +2... DOW: -6.38...ATT: -3...GM: -3.88...RADIO

OCTOBER

25

PRESIDENT HOOVER
RESPONDS

President Herbert Hoover took office in March 1929, when the stock market frenzy was at a fever pitch.

ON OCTOBER 25, in Washington, D.C., President Herbert Hoover was feeling frustrated. Reporters were calling and calling, demanding that he say something about the huge market decline the day before. Of course, the financial men wanted him to be reassuring. But the president, an engineer and businessman who had been in office just seven months, didn't share their confidence that the worst was over. He had been nervous about the stock market for months. On the other hand, he certainly did not want to make things worse. He would have to figure out the proper thing to say.

In a way, the huge decline of the last couple of days had been freakish. Every other panic in American history had started with some single crisis, such as the failure of a significant company or bank. But this time, no one event seemed to have triggered the reaction. The enemy here was too vague to identify by a single name.

Even before the market had grown shaky, President Hoover had been concerned. The thirty-first president had been inaugurated during a drenching rain in March. He promised to work for world peace, less crime, and an end to poverty. He hadn't mentioned the stock market then. But he wasn't happy that his predecessor, Calvin Coolidge, a leader known mostly for his silence, had assured the country during his last few days in office that stocks were "cheap at current prices."

"The stock boom was blowing great guns when I came into the

+1.75...ATT: -3.25...GM: +.50...RADIO: +2...STEEL: -1.80...DOW: +1.75...ATT: -3.25...GM: +.50...RA

White House," President Hoover wrote in his memoirs. Americans were taken with speculation. Investment was one thing; that meant buying a bond that paid interest or a stock with healthy profits that offered steady dividend payments from a company's profits. Companies with strong, growing businesses that produced real profits were the ones whose stocks should go up. Conservative investing was considered a wise use of money since one got real cash in return.

But speculation was a whole different concept. Speculators didn't care about dividends. They didn't care about profits. They didn't care whether a company's business was healthy or feeble. They bought on tips or hunches. Thousands bought the stock of Seaboard Air Line assuming it was an aviation company. In fact, it was a railroad. Speculators bought stocks only because they believed they would go up.

To President Hoover, "The real trouble was that the bellboys, the waiters, and the host of unknowing people, as well as the financial community, had become so obsessed with the constant press reports of great winnings that the movement was uncontrollable."

Or, in the words of Wall Street investment banker Otto H. Kahn, people "were determined that every piece of paper would be worth tomorrow twice what it was today."

Many investors were so certain that stocks would go up, they borrowed

No. 234				
Fiftieth National Bank				
DEMAND LOAN				
JENKINS & CO.				
$ 100,000.00				
Date August 16, 1929 Rate 6%				
Shares	SECURITIES	Price	Amount	
200	Southern Pacific	130	26	000
100	Canadian Pacific	222	22	200
100	U.S. Steel	150	15	000
500	U.S. Rubber	50	25	000
500	American Sugar Refining	76	38	000
1400			126	200

When an investor borrowed to buy shares, a bank tracked his loan and the value of his stock on an envelope. This investor borrowed $100,000 to buy shares in five companies for $126,000.

One of the hallmarks of the 1920s was the growth of the "easy payment plan." Originally developed to allow people to buy pricey items like houses and cars, the idea was simple. Buyers would put some money down and borrow the rest. They would pay off their loans in installments and pay interest charges for the use of the money. That way, people didn't have to save for years to afford a home or automobile.

In the 1920s, the idea spread to all kinds of items. An estimated 15 percent of retail sales—from clothes to jewelry to appliances—were made on the easy payment or installment plan. People from all kinds of backgrounds grew comfortable buying on credit.

Investors had long borrowed to buy stocks, but the amount they borrowed and the enthusiasm for borrowing took on a new meaning as the stock market boomed. Borrowing to buy a stock was different than buying a car on the installment plan. The initial payment was called margin. If the stock's price stayed the same or went up, the investor didn't have to pay another dime. The investor owned the stock and received any dividends from it. His broker, however, kept the stock certificate, which backed the loan. When the investor decided to sell his stock, his loan would be paid off along with interest charges and taxes, and he would get profit left over.

If the stock price fell, however, the investor would be asked to put up more margin to protect the broker's loan to him. If the investor didn't—or couldn't—add more cash, the stock would be sold. After the loan and interest charges were paid, the investor might not get anything. In fact, he might still owe money to the broker.

After making the stock purchase for the investor, the broker had to pay for the stock. Brokerages then took out their own loans. Often, they arranged a "call loan," a loan that could be "called" for repayment at any time.

money to buy them. One man, who told his story anonymously in *The American Magazine*, had been successful selling cars and had bought an automobile dealership. He was making a very comfortable $20,000 a year, when a rich customer insisted it was time the salesman "learned how to make money."

"Can you raise $10,000?" the customer inquired. The salesman had $4,000 in savings. He figured the bank would lend him $6,000 on his business. So, yes, he could do that.

"Buy yourself 500 shares of General Motors," the customer said. The salesman was shocked. General Motors was selling for more than $70 a share. That would be $35,000, almost two years' pay!

"That's all right," said the customer, and he gave the salesman the name of a broker.

A few days later, the salesman dropped into the broker's office, where the broker assured him that $10,000 in cash would be enough to buy $35,000 in General Motors stock. The cash portion would be his partial payment up front, which was called margin. The broker would lend him the other $25,000 at a reasonable interest rate. So in March, the salesman bought General Motors stock for about $70 a share.

By the end of September, the stock had climbed. The salesman bought more shares, this time without putting up one cent more. The value of his General Motors stock was so high that the broker was willing to lend him the full amount of his purchase. The stock was the collateral; that is, if the salesman couldn't repay the loan, the broker could take the stock and sell it. But who needed to worry about that? Didn't good stocks like General Motors mostly go up?

By the end of November, General Motors' stock had reached $140, double its price in March. The salesman sold half his shares. He repaid the bank for the loan he had taken on his business and he paid the broker part of what he owed on his stock loan. Even after that, he had $6,500 in cash to take home, more cash than he had started with.

Better, he still owned General Motors shares worth $35,000. All from a $4,000 start!

"Why, it sounds almost wicked," his wife said when he took her out to dinner to celebrate. "It *was* wicked," he wrote, "it was contrary to the moral law of the universe, which prescribes that a man shall earn his bread by the sweat of his brow." But who could pass up such a chance to get something for nothing?

By 1928, playing the stock market was so much more rewarding than selling cars that the salesman began to spend as much time at the broker's office as at his garage, stopping by morning, noon, and afternoon to check on the latest prices. When a visitor from the automobile maker questioned why he was away from work so often, the salesman took a hard look at his life. Not long before, he had spent most of a day trying to sell a customer a new car. Instead, he sold only a set of new bumpers, making a profit of $4. That same day, his stocks went up by $4,000. Any fool could see which was better. The salesman sold his business and began spending his days at his broker's office, watching stock prices.

The salesman thought he was very conservative. He sold some shares every time prices rose by a certain amount. By the fall of 1929, he had $70,000 in cash in the bank and $200,000 in stocks after subtracting what he owed the broker. But he was still in debt from buying stocks on margin and he owed his broker hundreds of thousands of dollars. In the heady days of 1928 and 1929, some brokers made loans if the buyer put down as little as $10 or $20 in cash for every $100 of stock.

For three years, the market mostly went up. Once or twice, the salesman had to add more margin—more cash—to protect his investment. That happened when prices fell and the broker felt that the stock he held wasn't enough to protect the stock loans. But each time, prices went back up. "Two steps up, one step down, two steps up

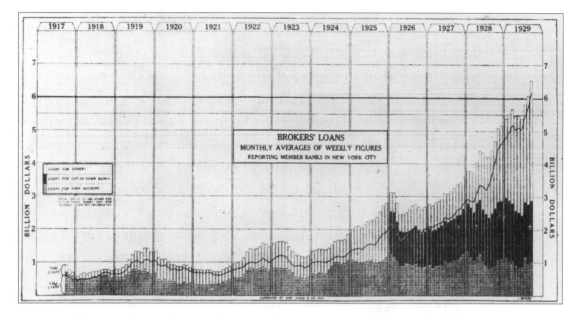

The amount of money borrowed to buy stocks soared in the late 1920s, as shown in this October 24, 1929, chart from *The Wall Street Journal.* The bottom bars indicate loans from New York banks. The dark bars in the middle indicate loans that New York banks made for out-of-town banks. The biggest jump came from New York banks' loans for others, like corporations.

again—that was how the market went"—or so people came to believe, wrote Frederick Lewis Allen, an astute observer of the day. That led to a logical conclusion, Mr. Allen said: "The really wise man, it appeared, was he who 'bought and held on.'"

It never occurred to the salesman that if prices dropped enough, even the money he had in the bank wouldn't be enough. The broker might take his bank savings and still sell all the salesman's stocks to cover his loans. The salesman could lose it all, and still owe money to the broker. But in the fall of 1929, that seemed as likely as putting a man on the moon.

When the salesman bought more stock and borrowed more from his broker, the broker, in turn, had to borrow to actually pay for the stock. What scared politicians and economists in the late 1920s was the way these brokers' loans multiplied, mirroring the growth in loans to stock buyers like the nameless salesman. At the end of 1927, New York

Stock Exchange brokers had more than $4 billion in outstanding loans from New York banks and others, an awesome level that was nearly $1 billion more than the year before. By the end of 1928, the brokers' loans had exploded to $6.4 billion, a 56 percent increase in one year.

Until this boom, companies had gone to banks to borrow money to build new plants or expand their branch offices. But with the public gobbling up stocks as avidly as they bought radios and cars, companies found it easy to sell shares to the public to raise money, rather than borrowing from banks. Millions of new shares were sold. That left banks with extra cash for loans, and they were all too happy to make loans to the people who wanted to buy all those new stocks. In fact, in 1929, nearly $4 of every $10 in bank loans was loaned for stocks.

To the men of the Federal Reserve, the nation's central bank, and to newly elected President Hoover, all this lending on stocks was frightful. When the music stopped and stocks went down instead of up, the borrowers might not be able to repay all those loans. Billions of dollars in loans could go bad, rocking the nation's financial system. Many people could go broke.

Early in 1929, the Federal Reserve tried to make it harder for banks to make loans on something as risky as stocks. But, President Hoover discovered, "the fever was beyond control." Almost as soon as he took office, President Hoover tried to tame the excitement. In March, he met with editors and publishers and asked them to use their editorials to warn the country about speculation. He sought out bankers and urged them to talk with their colleagues about their lending practices. He called Richard Whitney, vice president of the New York Stock Exchange, to Washington to see if he would rein in Stock Exchange members. "Mr. Whitney made profuse promises, but did nothing," President Hoover said.

The tug-of-war between Washington and Wall Street reached its peak in late March 1929. The Federal Reserve took steps to limit how much banks could lend for buying stocks. Interest rates doubled, which should have discouraged borrowing, "But people who dreamed of 100 percent profit in a week were not deterred by an interest rate of 20 percent a year," President Hoover recalled. "When the public becomes mad with greed and is rubbing the Aladdin's lamp of sudden fortune, no little matter of interest rates is effective." Borrowing continued.

At one point, the government nearly choked off the supply of loans for buying stock. In a single day in late March 1929, interest rates for stock loans jumped from 12 percent to 20 percent. For a time it looked as if money couldn't be borrowed for stocks at any price. On the New York Stock Exchange, stock prices "dropped like plummets."

The problem with borrowing to buy stocks was that everything could be lost if stock prices fell. In this 1929 drawing by well-known illustrator James Montgomery Flagg, the collapse in stock prices was especially painful for a borrowing family—including the housekeeper.

Life

On Margin.

JAMES MONTGOMERY FLAGG
Copyright 1929, LIFE Publishing Co.

The speculative bubble seemed poised to finally burst. "The back of the bull has been broken," traders told one another.

But the money men had other ideas. They were in no mood for a stock-market crash. Charles E. Mitchell, the outspoken chairman of National City Bank, for one, wouldn't let this bull market be ruined by what he saw as wrong-minded government types in Washington. The nerve of them! His bank, he announced on March 26, would "take steps to avert any dangerous crisis in the money market" by making loans to keep money flowing to Wall Street so speculators large and small could keep buying stocks on the partial-payment plan. The next day, he backed his words with numbers. National City would lend up to $25 million to brokers, he said.

The disaster was postponed. Stock prices turned.

To government officials, Congressmen, and others, Mr. Mitchell's action was appalling. The government had been trying to keep the speculation from getting completely out of hand. Mr. Mitchell wasn't just criticizing the government's efforts, he was undoing them. Senator Carter Glass of Virginia charged that Mr. Mitchell, "by extending aid to the market in a crisis had been guilty of slapping the Federal Reserve squarely in the face and of treating its policies with contempt." Mr. Mitchell seemed to

The Federal Reserve and government officials tried to tame stock market speculation in early 1929. But the public and Wall Street didn't want the ride to stop.

want the boom to continue no matter who got hurt or how badly.

Business leaders such as William C. Durant and other bankers who were profiting from the stock-market boom rallied around Mr. Mitchell. The criticism died down quickly. Wall Street, for the time being, had won the battle with Washington.

For the next few months, stock prices bounced up and down, but not strongly in either direction. Banks continued to make loans for stocks at relatively high interest rates. Then, in June, money for stock purchases loosened up. The new lenders? Corporations.

Companies saw that they could make nice profits on the money they lent for buying stocks, maybe more than the profits they could make selling cars or steel. Why turn down a sweet deal like that? At one point, Bethlehem Steel lent more than $157 million to speculators that might otherwise have gone to building or improving its businesses. John D. Rockefeller's Standard Oil Company of New Jersey, Chrysler Corporation, and General Motors also made tens of millions of dollars available for stock loans. In a perverse sort of circle, Cities Service Company, an energy company, sold some of its stock to the public. Then it took the cash from its stock sales and used it to make loans for people to buy stocks.

With money easier to get, the stock market took off again. As prices climbed, more speculators jumped in, greedy to catch the next wave. In an article in *Ladies' Home Journal* in August, John J. Raskob, a prominent businessman and Democratic leader, proclaimed, "Everybody ought to be rich." You only had to save $15 a month, every month, and invest it in stocks, he said. In twenty years, you would have a nest egg of $80,000! "And because anyone can do that, I am firm in my belief that anyone not only can be rich, but ought to be rich," he told his interviewer.

Over the summer, minor rumbles of trouble came from the nation's factories, but they couldn't be heard over the clamor for stocks. Steel

59

Everybody Ought to be Rich

An Interview With John J. Raskob

By SAMUEL CROWTHER

BEING rich is, of course, a comparative status. A man with a million dollars used to be considered rich, but so many people have at least that much in these days, or are earning incomes in excess of a normal return from a million dollars, that a millionaire does not cause any comment.

Fixing a bulk line to define riches is a pointless performance. Let us rather say that a man is rich when he has an income from invested capital which is sufficient to support him and his family in a decent and comfortable manner—to give as much support, let us say, as has ever been given by his earnings. That amount of prosperity ought to be attainable by anyone. A greater share will come to those who have greater ability.

It seems to me to be a primary duty for people to make it their business to understand how wealth is produced and not to take their ideas from writers and speakers who have the gift of words but not the gift of ordinary common sense. Wealth is not created in dens of iniquity, and it is much more to the point to understand what it is all about than to listen to the expounding of new systems which at the best can only make worse the faults of our present system.

It is quite true that wealth is not so evenly distributed as it ought to be and as it can be. And part of the reason for the unequal distribution is the lack of systematic investment and also the lack of even moderately sensible investment.

One class of investors saves money and puts it into savings banks or other mediums that pay only a fixed interest. Such funds are valuable, but they do not lead to wealth. A second class tries to get rich all at once, and buys any wildcat security that comes along with the promise of immense returns. A third class holds that the return from interest is not enough to justify savings, but at the same time has too much sense to buy fake stocks—and so saves nothing at all. Yet all the while wealth has been here for the asking.

The common stocks of this country have in the past ten years increased enormously in value because the business of the country has increased. Ten thousand dollars invested ten years ago in the common stock of General Motors would now be worth more than a million and a half dollars. And General Motors is only one of many first-class industrial corporations.

It may be said that this is a phenomenal increase and that conditions are going to be different in the next ten years. That prophecy may be true, but it is not founded on experience. In my opinion the wealth of the country is bound to increase at a very rapid rate. The rapidity of the rate will be determined by the increase in consumption, and under wise investment plans the consumption will steadily increase.

We Have Scarcely Started

NOW anyone may regret that he or she did not have ten thousand dollars ten years ago and did not put it into General Motors or some other good company—and sigh over a lost opportunity. Anyone who firmly believes that the opportunities are all closed and that from now on the country will get worse instead of better is welcome to the opinion—and to whatever increment it will bring. I think that we have scarcely started, and I have thought so for many years.

In conjunction with others I have been interested in creating and directing at least a dozen trusts for investment in equity securities. This plan of equity investment is no mere theory with me. The first of these trusts was started in 1907 and the others in the years immediately following. Under all of these the plan provided for the saving of fifteen dollars per month for investment in equity securities only. There were no stocks bought on margin, no money borrowed, nor any stocks bought for a quick turn or resale. All stocks with few exceptions have been bought and held as permanent investments. The fifteen dollars was saved every month and the dividends from the stocks purchased were kept in the trust and reinvested. Three of these trusts are now twenty years old. Fifteen dollars per month equals one hundred and eighty dollars a year. In twenty years, therefore, the total savings amounted to thirty-six hundred dollars. Each of these three trusts is now worth well in excess of eighty thousand dollars. Invested at 6 per cent interest, this eighty thousand dollars would give the trust beneficiary an annual income of four hundred dollars per month, which ordinarily would represent more than the earning power of the beneficiary, because had he been able to earn as much as four hundred dollars per month he could have saved more than fifteen dollars.

Suppose a man marries at the age of twenty-three and begins a regular saving of fifteen dollars a month—and almost anyone who is employed can do that if he tries. If he invests in good common stocks and allows the dividends and rights to accumulate, he will at the end of twenty years have at least eighty thousand dollars and an income from investments of around four hundred dollars a month. He will be rich. And because anyone can do that I am firm in my belief that anyone not only can be rich but ought to be rich.

The obstacles to being rich are two: The trouble of saving, and the trouble of finding a medium for investment. If Tom is known to have two hundred dollars in the savings bank then everyone is out to get it for some absolutely necessary purpose. More than likely his wife's sister will eventually find the emergency to draw it forth. But if he does withstand all attacks, what good will the money do him? The interest he receives is so small that he has no incentive to save, and since the whole is under his own jurisdiction he can depend only upon his own will to save. To save in any such fashion requires a stronger will than the normal.

If he thinks of investing in some stock he has nowhere to turn for advice. He is not big enough to get much attention from his banker, and he has not enough money to go to a broker—or at least he thinks that he has not.

Suppose he has ten thousand dollars; the bank can only advise him to buy a bond, for the officer will not take the risk of advising a stock and probably has not the experience anyway to give such advice. Tom can get really adequate attention only from some man who has a worthless security to sell, for then all of Tom's money will be profit.

The plan that I have had in mind for several years grows out of the success of the plans that we have followed for the executives in the General Motors and the Du Pont companies. In 1923, in order to give the executives of General Motors a greater interest in their work, we organized the Managers Securities Company, made up of eighty senior and junior executives. This company bought General Motors common stock to the then market value of thirty-three million dollars. The executives paid five million dollars in cash and borrowed twenty-eight million dollars. The stockholders of the Managers Securities Company are not stockholders in General Motors. They own stock in a company which owns stock in General Motors, so that, as far as General Motors is concerned, the stock is voted as a block according to the instructions of the directors of the Managers Securities Company. This supplies an important interest which can exercise a large influence in shaping the policies of General Motors.

From $25,000 to a Million

THE holdings of the members in the securities company are adjusted in cases of men leaving the employ of the company. The plan of the Managers Securities Company contemplates no dissolution of that company, so that its holdings of General Motors stock will always be en bloc. The plan has been enormously successful, and much of the success of the General Motors Corporation has been due to the executives' having full responsibility and receiving financial rewards commensurate with that responsibility.

The participation in the Managers Securities Company was arranged in accordance with the position and salary of the executive. Minimum participation required a cash payment of twenty-five thousand dollars when the Managers Securities Company was organized. That minimum participation is now worth more than one million dollars.

Recently I have been advocating the formation of an equity securities corporation; that is, a corporation that will invest in common stocks only under proper and careful supervision. This company will buy the common stocks of first-class industrial corporations and issue its own stock certificates against them. This stock will be offered from time to time at a price to correspond exactly with the value of the assets of the corporation and all profit will go to the stockholders. The directors will be men of outstanding character, reputation and integrity. At regular intervals—say quarterly—the whole financial record of the corporation will be published together with all of its holdings and the cost thereof. The corporation will be owned by the public and with every transaction public. I am not at all interested in a private investment trust. The corporation would not be permitted to borrow money or go into any debt.

In addition to this company, there should be organized a discount company on the same lines as the finance companies

(Continued on Page 56)

Ladies' Home Journal captured the prevalent attitude of 1929: *Anyone* who invested in stocks could be wealthy down the road.

production was down. Automobile sales were falling. Fewer houses were being built. People were losing their jobs. But those seemed like minor bumps.

Even the most alert financial publications failed to see any signs of slowdown. In fact, many of them were trying to grab a piece of this golden age themselves. *Business Week* magazine made its debut in September 1929. *The Wall Street Journal* launched its Pacific Coast edition on October 21, 1929. Time, Inc., already was advertising its new deluxe business magazine, *Fortune,* which would hit newsstands in January.

Demand for stocks had never been so good. Between May and September, 60 companies sold stock on the New York Stock Exchange, adding more than 100 million new shares to the marketplace.

As speculators bought more stocks, they borrowed more and more. Economist John Kenneth Galbraith observed, "it seemed as though Wall Street were by way of devouring all the money of the entire world." Stock prices peaked on September 3, when the Dow Jones Industrial Average hit 381.17, up 27 percent since the end of 1928. But even when stock prices began to slowly ratchet down, the amount of loans for stock purchases grew. Loans to New York Stock Exchange brokers reached $8.5 billion in October, a gargantuan gain of nearly $2 billion in five months.

To President Hoover, it was "an orgy of speculation." Stock prices were too high, he was sure, and the painful declines of October 23 and October 24 were long overdue. Even if he believed this with all his heart, however, on October 25, he had to come up with something more cheerful and reassuring to say to the American people.

The president finally settled on a statement with all the spice of a bowl of oatmeal: "The fundamental business of the country, that is production and distribution of commodities, is on a sound and prosperous basis." The president noted that production and consumption were at high levels, worker wages and productivity were increasing,

Investment firms that relied on investors to buy stocks ran ads calling for calm and encouraging people not to overreact to the downturn.

and other factors looked good. He made no mention at all of stocks or stock prices.

The comment hardly wowed the markets, but it didn't scare them either. By Thursday's standards, Friday, October 25, was a relatively calm day. "Wall Street scrambled to its feet, felt its throbbing head, put a fresh carnation in its buttonhole and went back to work," the New York *World* reported.

Nearly 6 million shares changed hands, but much of the distress selling had disappeared. The Dow Jones Industrial Average actually closed up a bit. The bankers' help wasn't needed much on Friday. There were buyers for most of the shares being sold.

Trading was still heavy, and brokers and traders struggled to catch their collective breath. Some sense of stability returned. *The New York Times* ventured so far as to predict, "the market is once more on an even keel." A few even managed to laugh. Friday night at the annual meeting of the American Iron and Steel Institute, steel magnate Charles M. Schwab began, "It would probably be quite correct for me to start my remarks to you with the words, 'Friends and former millionaires.'"

: +1.75...ATT: -3.25...GM: +.50...RADIO: +2...STEEL: -1.80...DOW: +1.75...ATT: -3.25...GM: +.50...

OCTOBER

26

SOLD OUT

THE MARKETS MAY have been faring better, but the little investors, the individuals, were hurting. Thursday's crash had so hammered stock prices that many small-time speculators were in deep trouble. Brokers were demanding more cash. If the little guys couldn't deliver more money, their stocks would be sold and their savings would be gone.

The situation was so grim that a dark humor rose out of it. Eddie Cantor, a vaudeville comedian and singer, lost his savings and had only the $60 in his pocket. But he was quick to make light of it. After stocks fell so sharply, he said he went to a hotel in New York and asked for a room on the nineteenth floor. "The clerk looked up at me and

ABOVE: Though usually quiet on a Saturday, cars and people crowded the financial district as the stock market tried to stabilize.

asked: 'What for? Sleeping or jumping?'" Then there was the joke about two men who jumped from a bridge together. Why? They had a joint account.

For many, though, the experience was far from humorous. Groucho Marx, possibly one of the funniest men in America, was in a dark and painful funk. His stocks, representing his life's savings, had fallen along with the broader market, and the calls for more cash were coming fast and furious.

The first one had come at 9 A.M. earlier in the week. His broker was on the phone and sounding urgent. "There's been a slight break in the market, Mr. Marx. You'd better get down here with some cash to cover your margin."

"I thought I was covered," Mr. Marx responded, still shaking off a deep sleep.

"Not enough for the way things are going," the broker told him. "We'll need more. And you'd better hurry!"

In the past week, tens of thousands of such calls had been made. Though it seemed like many more at the time, only an estimated six hundred thousand people actually had margin accounts in 1929. The week's events had put pressure on many of them. The first large round of calls for more cash had gone out about a week before; many, many more calls went out after prices dropped on Monday. By the time prices really started to sink on Wednesday and

The comedian Eddie Cantor included this cartoon in a book lampooning the stock market crash. This joke became a trademark of the 1929 crash.

"I want a room on the nineteenth floor."
"What for? Sleeping or jumping?"

Thursday, many small speculators had just about run out of ways to come up with cash. A good bit of the selling on Thursday, it was believed, came from brokers dumping the stocks of customers who were in debt and could not deliver more cash.

Brokers made loans assuming that a stock was valuable enough to repay the loan. A customer might buy $10,000 in stock, paying $2,500 in cash and borrowing $7,500 from his broker. If the stock's value fell

WHAT IS A BROKERAGE HOUSE?

The word "broker" comes from the French word *brocour*, an intermediary who bought large containers of wine, intending to sell it by the bottle or glass. Stockbrokers are middlemen who help people buy and sell stock. An investor who wants to buy shares calls a stockbroker, who makes sure the stock is purchased. For the service, the investor pays a commission, or fee based on the size of the purchase.

In the 1920s most brokerage houses were small, handling the stock accounts of family members and acquaintances. The largest brokerage houses were sometimes called commission houses and employed "customers' men" to help investors make their stock purchases and sales. The commission houses often had customers' rooms decorated as libraries, where clients sat in comfortable chairs to read financial publications, observe the ticker tape, and watch young clerks write the latest stock prices on blackboards.

When a customer placed an order, the customer's man would write up the request on a slip of paper, and the order would be passed on to the brokerage house's representative on the Stock Exchange floor.

In some ways, brokerage houses also acted like banks in an era when deposits could disappear if a traditional bank failed. Brokerage houses took deposits from customers, made loans so customers could buy stocks, and held on to cash until the customer decided what to buy. Customers got copies of their accounts, which were kept by hand in large ledger books.

W: -2.25...ATT: +.25...GM: +.25...RADIO: -1.63...STEEL: -.63...DOW: -2.25...ATT: +.25...GM: +.25...F

From the October 26 New York *World* came another bittersweet look at the financial pain caused by the stock market drop.

Can You Lend Me A Nickel To Get Home On ?

to $8,000, the customer's margin—the stock value minus his loan—would fall to $500. The stock's value would still cover the loan, but not by very much.

Brokers needed more cash from customers when prices fell sharply. They couldn't wait for prices to fall so far that their loans could not be paid back. Without more cash from the customer, the broker had to sell the shares.

Because stock prices seemed to climb so effortlessly in the late 1920s, many first-time investors had no idea how suddenly their fortunes could change. They had never seen prices collapse suddenly and then fall even farther. When their brokers called for more cash, they scrambled to provide it. They fully expected prices to go back up again, restoring their profits. They couldn't imagine the day when stocks didn't recover, nor did they anticipate the shock and pain they would feel when they realized that both their cash and their investments were gone.

The stock-market fever caught on with all kinds of people, from the young and ambitious to retirees looking to supplement their pensions. Working-class men and top professionals bet on the hottest stocks. Worldly politicians like Winston Churchill and many of the day's most famous entertainers joined in too. When prices fell, many of them shared the same agony. Famous as he was, Groucho Marx was among the most candid about his situation—and the funniest, too.

Like so many others, Groucho didn't see the risks ahead when he started buying stocks. He believed the market was a safe and sound place. After all, the truly rich, such as the Morgans, the Whitneys, and the Du Ponts, didn't buy their yachts with the interest from their bank accounts. They put their money to work for them in stocks. Groucho especially liked buying on margin. His broker made it so easy to get a loan. "It was like stealing money," he said.

The actor didn't have a financial adviser because he didn't need one. "You could close your eyes, stick your finger any place on the Big Board and the stock you had just bought would start rising," he said. He took advice from almost anyone. A friend recommended Auburn Auto, saying, "this is a fast rider. It will jump like a kangaroo." So Groucho bought five hundred shares. Just before a matinee perform-ance, his brother Chico heard from a Wall Street tipster that Anaconda Copper would fly to $500 a share from a mere $138. Brothers Chico, Harpo, and Groucho called their broker and kept an audience waiting for thirty minutes to be sure they were lucky enough to buy two hun-dred shares each.

Perhaps Groucho's most foolish investment was made the day he took a tip from an elevator man at the Copley Plaza Hotel in Boston. The elevator man told him of some big shots wearing the latest double-breasted suits and carnations in their buttonholes. One big shot told the other to buy all he could of United Corporation.

Groucho gave the elevator man a tip and ran to tell Harpo, who was still in his bathrobe, about the stock they should buy. "There's a broker's office in the lobby," Harpo told him. "Wait'll I get my clothes on and we'll go downstairs and grab this stock before news of it gets around."

"Are you crazy?" Groucho retorted. "If we wait until you get your

68

A young Groucho Marx studies the financial pages. Without his trademark moustache, he was rarely recognized.

clothes on, that stock may jump ten points." So Harpo in his bathrobe and Groucho in a hurry rushed to the broker's office and placed an order.

As quickly as he could decide to buy, Groucho could never seem to let go, even when his stocks climbed very high. "The little judgment I had told me to sell, but like all the other suckers, I was greedy," he said. "I was loath to relinquish any stock that was sure to double in a few months."

Groucho yearned for the financial comfort that his stocks promised. Like many immigrants, Groucho had a large family, and money had been very tight. Once, when he was twelve, he remembered eyeing a sweet roll all through dinner. There never seemed to be enough food to go around, and he couldn't work up the nerve to reach for it. Finally, when he thought his brothers weren't looking, he slid his hand along the table and onto the platter. Just then, Harpo grabbed a meat cleaver and swung. Groucho pulled away quickly. Rather than catch his brother's hand, Harpo shattered the platter and put the cleaver halfway into the table. Even worse, their Uncle Julius got the roll.

Groucho made up his mind then that he would find a way to earn enough money to live comfortably. And, he pledged, he would handle his money carefully so he would never have to worry about fighting

for the last sweet roll. His mother, Minnie, pushed and prodded Groucho and three of his brothers to start a singing act. Unfortunately, they weren't very good—but they *were* very funny. With a combination of music, skits, and humor, the Marx Brothers—Groucho, Harpo, Chico, and Zeppo—evolved into one of the greatest comedy acts of all time.

In the late 1920s the brothers were touring the East Coast in the show *Animal Crackers,* their biggest hit to date. Groucho, with his trademark greasepaint mustache and fat cigar, and Harpo, playing a wig-wearing, girl-chasing mute, each were making an impressive two thousand dollars a week. Both had been able to sock away nearly a quarter of a

At the time of the stock market crash, the Marx Brothers were touring the country in the musical comedy *Animal Crackers.*

million dollars, all of which they had put in stocks.

By fall 1929, Groucho was thrilled with how well his stocks were doing. But he was nervous, too. In early October he had asked his broker how stocks could keep going up and up, especially when some of the companies like Radio didn't even pay a dividend. "Shouldn't there be some relation between a company's earnings, its dividends and the stock's selling price?" he said.

The broker smirked. It would be hard for a non-financial man like Mr. Marx to understand, the broker answered. But, he assured his client, "This has ceased to be a national market. We're now in a world market." The possibilities, the broker insisted, were endless.

Groucho's brother, Harpo, also infatuated with the stock market, played a mute, girl-chasing professor in the comedy.

71

But in late October, prices began to fall and Groucho got the phone call asking for more margin. When he arrived at the broker's office in Great Neck, New York, that day, ticker tape was knee-deep on the floor. Some people were frantically trying to sell. Others were scribbling checks to meet margin calls. In a vain effort to keep the broker from selling his stocks, Groucho gave him all the cash he had.

Even though trading on the New York Stock Exchange was orderly and steady on Saturday, October 26, brokers were still selling the depressed stocks of customers who could no longer meet their margin calls. Some big stocks like General Electric and Western Union slid $8 and $10 a share as customers' stocks were dumped on the market for whatever price they would bring. Brokerage firms were so behind in their bookkeeping that many still didn't have a good handle on what their customers had and how much they owed. Under different circumstances, the Stock Exchange might have closed to give clerks and record-keepers a chance to catch up. But no one wanted to send the wrong message and scare the public further.

Alfred P. Sloan, the president of General Motors, saw a bright spot in the gloomy series of events. The slump is a healthy thing, he told reporters as he boarded a ship in London to return home. "Now everybody will get to work instead of cherishing the idea that it is possible to get rich overnight by speculation."

Groucho Marx tried to see a bright spot too, but it was difficult. Late in the week, he had to come up with even more cash. Auburn Auto, which had sold for as much as $514 earlier that year, was now down to $215. Radio was trading at half its highest price for the year. To raise cash, Groucho borrowed money from the bank. He borrowed on his life insurance policy. He took a mortgage loan on his home.

Even that additional cash wouldn't be enough. His broker sold all his stocks. All of his precious savings were gone. And he was badly in debt.

The Marx Brothers were to open *Animal Crackers* in Baltimore on

Monday, but Groucho, who had never been a happy man, was now truly depressed. He didn't feel very funny. He wasn't sure he wanted to make people laugh—or that he could. His brothers and the producer tried to coax him to go on. But Groucho was too deeply in mourning. An understudy had to handle the first four performances. One newspaper said the star was "down in the back with a misery"—apparently, the misery of Wall Street.

Groucho's severe depression lasted for months, but he returned to the stage in a few days, his usual sarcasm now aimed at his own disaster. In his entrance as Captain Spaulding, an explorer who has just

New York *World* cartoonist Rollin Kirby captured the despair of the small-time investor who saw his stocks "sold out" and his savings lost on October 24.

returned from wrestling polar bears in Africa, he was carried in on a sedan chair. Ad-libbing, he turned to one of his carriers and pointed to the sedan. "Take this out and sell it," he said. "I just got word from my broker that he wants more margin." The audience cracked up. More stock-market jokes followed, until the crowd and his brothers were in hysterics.

"Some of the people I know lost millions," he wrote in his autobiography. Composer Irving Berlin, for one, lost about $5 million. But, said Groucho, "I was luckier. All I lost was two hundred and forty thousand dollars. (Or one hundred and twenty weeks of work at two thousand per.) I would have lost more but that was all the money I had."

At least he had steady, reliable work. Many other naïve investors found themselves in financial holes so deep that they had to sell their cars, their jewelry, and their homes. Their future, once so bright, was now terribly grim.

-2.25...ATT: +.25...GM: +.25...Radio: -1.63...Steel: -.63...Dow: -2.25...ATT: +.25...GM:

OCTOBER

27

THE KING OF
THE BULLS

THE LAST FEW DAYS had been as hard on the big boys as on the little guys. Except for a few men who had seen trouble coming and sold most of their holdings, many large speculators had suffered multi-million-dollar losses. The financial houses, still struggling to get their account books in order, were full of rumors that some of the biggest names on Wall Street might be on their last legs.

Whether that was true would be hard to tell until all those records were straightened out. For the first time ever, Mike Meehan and his team had to join other specialists at their posts from 10 A.M. to 1 P.M. on a Sunday to fix disagreements and clear up confused orders on their books. So many people were working on the New York Stock Exchange floor that only the lack of clicking ticker gave away that the Exchange was actually closed.

Usually deserted on Sundays, the sidewalks of the financial district were filled with rushing messengers on October 27. Automobiles were parked in double rows along Broad Street, Broadway, and other nearby streets. Tour buses detoured to show sightseers where all the money had been lost. Some visitors walked the area hoping to find a stray piece of ticker tape as a souvenir.

In brokers' offices, exhausted clerks had been working around the clock and were still behind. Hotels and gymnasiums put up cots in open spaces and hallways so the thousands of Wall Street workers could try to catch a few hours' sleep. Restaurants made special arrangements to remain open. Men handling the books and women working at adding machines and typewriters fainted at their desks from pure fatigue. When possible, they were revived and put back to work, though some businesses finally had to send workers home. As the numbers were tallied, it was clear that many more customers were likely to be wiped out in coming days.

But William C. Durant—Billy to his closest friends—was upbeat as usual. In his many years buying and selling stocks, he had seen quite a

few ups and downs. True, this drop was more severe. But the "King of the Bulls" was so thoroughly opinionated and so relentlessly confident—such a genuine bull—that he just assumed the drop was temporary and stocks would be riding upward before long.

Wall Street was usually closed on Sundays, but firms were way behind on paperwork. The men of Harriman and Company worked through the day to catch up on transactions.

Mr. Durant had to be an optimist to have gotten where he was. At sixty-seven years old, he had experienced more failure than most people could endure, and bounced back each time. Now he was considered one of the biggest and most powerful players in the stock market.

A small man with tufts of fuzzy gray hair and an impish twinkle in his eyes, William C. Durant had grown up in Flint, Michigan, and quit school at seventeen. He dabbled in a number of jobs, working in a lumberyard, managing the city's waterworks, and selling insurance. In 1886, he happened across a horse-drawn carriage with a special springy seat that softened the bumpy ride on dirt roads. Impressed, he tracked down the inventor and offered to buy the design. With a partner, he formed the Durant-Dort Carriage Company and helped change the way Americans move about.

William C. Durant made his first two fortunes in transportation before he turned his attention to the stock market.

Mr. Durant had a natural talent for sales. So persuasive that he was said to charm the birds out of trees, he traveled the region talking up the Durant-Dort comfortable carriage. By 1904, Durant-Dort Carriage Company was one of the largest carriage makers in the United States, and Billy Durant was a millionaire. But to the bewilderment of his coworkers, he was off chasing another new idea: the automobile.

Though he initially thought autos were noisy, smelly, and dangerous, Mr. Durant had come to believe that the horseless carriage would one day own the roads. He backed an automobile entrepreneur named David Buick and then bought a small manufacturer called Olds, later called Oldsmobile. In 1908, he put them together in a company he named General Motors. Others laughed at Mr. Durant's dream and his enthusiasm for the motorcar. They had another name for General Motors: "Durant's folly."

But Billy Durant, cocky and sure of himself, pushed forward. He bought twenty more companies over two years, including Cadillac, a company later to be called Pontiac, body plants, and accessory factories. He was so busy and working so hard that he sometimes scheduled appointments for 1 A.M. At one point, he agreed to buy Ford Motor from Henry Ford. But his banks balked at lending the money, and the deal fell through.

In 1910, the economy turned down. General Motors' sales, which had reached almost $50 million in just two years, started to fall. Mr. Durant's company was overextended. It had made too many cars and had too many commitments. He needed a quick $15 million. Bankers ultimately gave it to him, but at a huge price: They took control of General Motors away from him.

Mr. Durant lost his shareholder's right to vote for company directors and other matters for five years. He left with only a little of his wealth intact. But he didn't venture far. Never one to dawdle, he quickly convinced race-car driver Louis Chevrolet to help him start another car company. The Chevrolet car sold well enough to get Mr. Durant back in business.

Mr. Durant still owned General Motors shares and he wanted to get back at the wheel of his old company. Once a year, shareholders get to vote for their company's directors, with each share counting as one vote. After five years had passed, Mr. Durant could again control his shares. He convinced his friends who were General Motors' shareholders to support his efforts to return. In 1915, according to General Motors lore—which was probably exaggerated—Mr. Durant stood up in front of the automaker's executives and directors and declared, "I am in control of General Motors today." By 1916 he was again running General Motors, his baby.

As a leader, the quirky Mr. Durant was a one-man show. Formal and always well-dressed, his colleagues called him W. C., not the familiar Billy. He disapproved of smoking or drinking, and kept his office windows closed to keep out fresh air. His meals were delivered from home. Sometimes he would carry on three different meetings in three different rooms, running between them. In the mornings, full of nervous energy, he would bark orders from his folding barber's chair as an attendant shaved and snipped. He worked weekends and holidays. At the same time, he would stop almost anything for a game of checkers, sometimes playing for hours, and he remained fascinated by the stock market, buying and selling on the side.

General Motors executives predicted a huge boom in sales after the World War. The company planned a tremendous expansion, borrowing heavily to build new plants and produce more automobiles. But a small depression, not an expansion, followed. Auto sales fell. To Billy Durant's horror, General Motors' stock price fell too. Mr. Durant began to buy the stock with his own money to push the price up. No matter how many shares he bought, however, the price continued to drop.

By the time the dust settled in late 1920, Billy Durant suffered one of the largest single losses in stock market history. Over several months, he spent and lost his entire fortune of $90 million trying to prop up General Motors shares. For the second time in roughly ten years, both he and the company were deeply in debt.

To save both of them, representatives of the J. P. Morgan Company and Du Pont, the explosives and chemical company, stepped in. They provided new funds for General Motors, and they bought Mr. Durant's GM shares for just enough money to pay off his debts and keep him afloat. Once again, he was thrown out of the company he founded— and this time, it was for good.

Given his experiences, Mr. Durant could have disappeared in shame. He could have retired peacefully. But, as a close associate once observed, "You know, W. C. is never happy unless he is hanging to a window sill by his finger tips." Mr. Durant was too single-minded to stop playing the power-and-money games he loved so much. "Forget mistakes. Forget failures," he told a reporter in 1921. "Forget everything except what you're going to do now and do it. Today is your lucky day."

He formed yet another car company, Durant Motors. The company produced a few popular cars, but it wasn't well-run and it never made solid profits. Mr. Durant wasn't as involved as he had been before.

Almost since they began, stock and bond markets have attracted professional investors ready to take tremendous financial risks in the hopes of making a fortune. Often called "speculators" or "plungers," these market pros are willing to borrow heavily to buy large quantities of stocks or bonds. The nation's first treasury secretary, Alexander Hamilton, was so appalled at one early investor that he wrote in 1792, "'Tis time there should be a line of separation between honest Men & knaves, between respectable Stockholders and dealers in the funds, and more unprincipled Gamblers."

Wall Street has long struggled to find that proper line. In the heady days of the late 1920s, some of the biggest plungers openly used manipulation and deceit to turn a profit. They formed pools, or groups of wealthy investors, to buy a certain stock.

Pool members hoped to get the public so excited about a stock that smaller investors would buy the stock, pushing up the price. Often the pool hired promoters to talk about the stock on the radio or write glowing articles for newspapers. The public did not know that the information had been purchased; they only heard a man on the radio talking about Maxwell Motors or read glowing stories about Superior Oil Corporation. In exchange for publishing stories provided by publicity men, financial writers from dozens of respected newspapers, including *The New York Times* and *The Wall Street Journal*, accepted payments of cash or stock.

Little investors, reading in stock gossip columns about a pool's interest in a company, tried to play along. If smart professionals were buying, they should be buying too, they figured. But the pools had one piece of information that small investors didn't have: when to sell. One big Wall Street trader predicted the result to *The New York Times*: "Stock Exchange history pretty well proves that this sort of traders, who have no business in the market in the first place, usually have the stocks and some one else has the money when all the excitement is over."

Instead, working in a New York City office about twenty minutes from Wall Street, with three or four phones at his elbow, the Eternal Bull was putting his endless energy into buying and selling stocks.

As other market players saw his success, he began to invest his friends' money too. By 1927, brokers' stock-market reports referred to a "Durant market," saying Mr. Durant's investments were affecting the whole market. The public began to listen to his optimistic song, following him like the Pied Piper.

By now, Mr. Durant was investing hundreds of millions of dollars. Among his sometime-partners were other men who made their fortunes in autos, like the seven Fisher brothers, who sold their family's auto-body company to General Motors for $200 million. There was Arthur Cutten of Chicago, who made millions trading in grain. Mr. Cutten once cornered the wheat market, a move that supposedly gave him control of more grain than any man since Joseph in Egypt. Now focused on stocks, the businessmen were so bullish, so intent on making sure

In the early 1920s, after leaving General Motors for the second time, Billy Durant started Durant Motors. Here, with a colleague, he inspects new Durant automobiles.

that the market would go up, that they were nicknamed "the Midwest prosperity boys."

Newspapers estimated Mr. Durant's personal worth at $100 million. The investor boasted that his winning method was easy. He studied a company's business and its prospects carefully before buying. "I have tried to find meritorious stocks selling far below their real worth, and then I've backed them with my judgment," he said.

That sounded rational enough. But truth be told, Mr. Durant and his fellow "plungers" mostly bought stocks they thought they could push upward. Their classic method was to line up a secret "syndicate," or group of wealthy like-minded investors. By pooling their money and

WHAT IS A STOCK SPLIT?

When a company's stock rises over time, it sometimes becomes too expensive for small investors to buy it. To make the stock more affordable, company boards of directors will declare a "stock split," offering two or three or more new shares for every old share. When two new shares replace every one share currently available, the number of outstanding shares increases and the share price is adjusted downward.

In the 1920s, companies liked splits because they were a kind of magic trick, an illusion. The idea is much like cutting a pie into more and more pieces; in the end, you still have the same pie. For example, a company's stock might trade at $100 a share. A shareholder who owned ten shares would have stock valued at $1,000. If the company split the shares four-for-one, it would give shareholders four new shares for every one share they owned, and the price would change to $25 a share. The shareholder now would have forty shares, but the shares would still have a value of $1,000.

Unsophisticated buyers get excited about stock splits, thinking they are getting a better deal because the stock price is cheaper. They will buy the shares hoping the price will automatically climb back to where it was before the split. Usually, though, stock prices rise for better reasons than sleight-of-hand, such as growing demand for a company's goods or fatter profits.

carefully buying and selling, this group of Wall Street insiders could move a stock around like a marionette to lure the public to buy.

In 1929, wealthy Wall Street insiders such as Billy Durant ran pools in

Debit Date 1929	Securities	Shares	Purchases	Receipts	Memorandum	Interest	Cash	Misc.	Folio	Total
Mar					7/30 - Tfr to Copper Stock Trading A/c (Contra)			505 0 0 0		
Apr	Chrysler	500	46 78 7 50							
	Nat'l Cash Register	12 500		1 76 6 76 6 05	4/9 70 A/c					
					4/9 - 70 A/c Payment against Participation (Contra)			510 2 0 0		
					7/30 - Tfr from A/c 418 A/c Rose			40 5 4 05		
						44 2 5 30				
										10 65 3 81
May	Warner Bros.	11,000	14 16 70 4 50							
	Inter. Comb. Eng.	1 000	77 1 25							
	Nat Cash Register									
	Chrysler									
	Nat Cash Register									
June					To Chk Whittier		86 99 0 35			
July	Warner Bros	3000	18 80 75			9 28 72				
	Chrysler	500	36 21 2 50							
	Inter. Comb. Eng.	1900	12 96 3 2 50							
	Nat Cash Register									
	Warner Bros.	2000		— 0 —	7/18 Whittier					
	Industrial Rayon	500		— 0 —	7/18 "					
		32 900	18 84 5 37	1 76 6 76 6 05		16 0 07 82	86 99 0 35	10 15 0 54 05		

more than one hundred stocks. One of the most famous was in Radio stock in March 1929, exactly one year after the high-flier caught the nation's attention. In 1928, Radio's stock had climbed as high as $420 a share. By early March 1929, the shares were back down to $370. To make the stock seem more affordable, Radio executives had announced they would split it five-for-one in late March, giving each shareholder five shares for every one owned. The new stock was trading on the New York Stock Exchange at around $74 a share.

Delivered	Memorandum	Cash	Interest	Misc.	Dividend	Total	Folio	Balance	Collateral
	3/28 - Whittier Corp Profit from Radio Participation			505000 - n					
	4/3 - % Radio Synd			738076					
	4/3 - Ifv from Copper Stock Trading % (Contra)			505000 - n					
	4/11 - Ifv from #70.% (Contra)			510000 - n					
	4/12 - Ifv from Radio Synd. 4/30 - Ifv from %+418 F 4/12 - 12700 N.C. Reg.			430354 2210583	9525 -			12737177	12500 N.C. Reg 500 Chrysler
670000 -	5/15 Beny Hill								
202878 -	5/27 P.F. Cusack							8691792	
			7243					- 0 -	
50									
350								2775837	5000 Warner 500 Ind. Rayon 1500 Int. C. Eng. Short: 100 Nat C Reg

Unknown to little investors, Wall Street's big insiders had a plan. Behind the scenes, Mike Meehan sent a confidential letter on March 7 to more than fifty traders and prominent businessmen, such as Walter Chrysler and Charles Schwab. Mr. Meehan said he had been asked to form a syndicate to trade in up to 1 million shares of Radio. Would they like to join in? It was hard to pass up a

Mr. Durant kept track of his many stock purchases and sales in large leather-bound ledger books. These pages from 1929 show his investments with M. J. Meehan and Co. and profits from participating in the 1929 Radio Corporation pool.

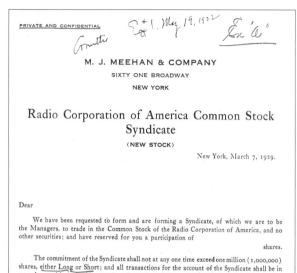

M. J. MEEHAN & COMPANY

SIXTY ONE BROADWAY

NEW YORK

Radio Corporation of America Common Stock Syndicate

(NEW STOCK)

New York, March 7, 1929.

Dear

We have been requested to form and are forming a Syndicate, of which we are to be the Managers, to trade in the Common Stock of the Radio Corporation of America, and no other securities; and have reserved for you a participation of

shares.

The commitment of the Syndicate shall not at any one time exceed one million (1,000,000) shares, either Long or Short; and all transactions for the account of the Syndicate shall be in accordance with, and subject to the rules and regulations of the New York Stock Exchange.

Subject only to the limitations aforesaid, the Managers, in a trading account on the books of Messrs. M. J. Meehan & Company, who are hereby appointed Agents for the Managers, entitled "Radio Corporation of America Common Stock Syndicate" shall have full power and authority, hereby granted, in their uncontrolled judgment and discretion during the life and for the account of the Syndicate to buy, sell and generally trade in the Common Stock of the Radio Corporation of America, either Long or Short, and at or through public or private sale, and to deal in "puts" and "calls" thereon.

The profits and the losses of the Syndicate shall be divided among and borne by the participants in proportion to their respective participation. The participants shall be deemed to participate in each transaction in proportion to their several interests in the Syndicate. Any loss resulting from the failure of any participant to carry out his or her obligation hereunder shall not be charged as a loss to the Syndicate; but in respect of any such loss incurred or threatened resulting from such failure, the Managers shall have full power and authority, hereby granted, to take such action by sale or otherwise, and with or without notice as in their uncontrolled discretion is necessary to protect the Managers and the Syndicate against loss.

Fifty prominent investors received this letter inviting them to join a special "syndicate," or pool in Radio Corporation's stock. Those who participated made thousands of dollars in just a few days.

shindig like this one, and the invited hurried to accept. The wife of Radio Corporation president David Sarnoff got ten thousand shares and she didn't have to put up a dime. Neither did three of the Fisher brothers, who signed up for twenty thousand shares. Billy Durant took one of the biggest pieces, twenty-five thousand shares, and made a deposit of $400,000. That was a bargain: At the price of the new shares, Mr. Durant's stake in the pool should have cost about $2 million.

While everyone's signatures were being gathered, Radio shares started to climb. On Monday, March 11, 1929, the *New York Daily News,* in its trading gossip column, predicted Radio "should be a real buy" on Tuesday. *The Wall Street Journal,* which had run two glowing stories on the company in recent days, reported that Radio shares "were the sensation of the market last week," thanks to "the formation of a new bull pool."

The pool officially began operating the next day, with Mike Meehan making trades that helped the ticker tell exciting stories about Radio stock. Over the next few days—around the time President Hoover was lecturing newspaper editors about stock market excesses—thousands of Radio shares were traded back and forth between the

: -2.25...ATT: +.25...GM: +.25...RADIO: -1.63...STEEL: -.63...DOW: -2.25...ATT: +.25...GM: +.25...RA

RADIO CORPORATION OF AMERICA AND SUBSIDIARY COMPANIES

CONSOLIDATED BALANCE SHEET AT DECEMBER 31, 1929

ASSETS

CURRENT ASSETS:

Cash in Banks and on Hand		$ 15,318,506.19
Marketable Securities at Cost (December 31, 1929 Market Value in excess of Cost)		16,811,292.12
Notes and Accounts Receivable less Reserves		26,732,554.15
Inventories at Cost or Market less Reserves		31,946,797.78
TOTAL CURRENT ASSETS		$ 90,809,150.24

INVESTMENTS:

Securities, Notes of and Advances to Associated and Other Companies, less Reserves		33,032,683.85

FIXED ASSETS:

Factories, Radio Communication and Broadcasting Stations, Warehouses, Service Shops, Offices, etc.—Land, Buildings and Equipment in Operation and Construction	$57,467,904.02	
LESS: Reserves	24,381,490.36	
	$33,086,413.67	
Patents, Contracts and Goodwill	444,866.91	
TOTAL FIXED ASSETS		33,531,280.58

DEFERRED CHARGES:

Taxes, Insurance, etc. paid in advance		1,306,768.93
TOTAL ASSETS		$158,679,883.60

RADIO CORPORATION OF AMERICA AND SUBSIDIARY COMPANIES

CONSOLIDATED BALANCE SHEET AT DECEMBER 31, 1929

LIABILITIES AND CAPITAL

CURRENT LIABILITIES:

Current Accounts Payable	$33,792,723.07	
Accrued Federal Income Taxes	1,730,970.87	
Miscellaneous Accruals and Payables	1,304,636.83	
Dividends Declared and Unpaid	1,309,254.03	
TOTAL CURRENT LIABILITIES		$ 38,137,584.80

FUNDED DEBT AND OTHER LIABILITIES:

Advance by General Electric Company and Westinghouse Electric & Manufacturing Company through Audio Vision Appliance Company	$32,000,000.00	
Mortgages Payable	1,791,416.67	
Notes Payable (Serial Notes maturing $50,000 annually)	907,009.85	
TOTAL FUNDED DEBT AND OTHER LIABILITIES		34,698,426.52

RESERVES:

General Reserve	$ 2,600,000.00	
Other Reserves	890,851.59	
TOTAL RESERVES		3,490,851.59

CAPITAL STOCK:

"A" Preferred—7%— Par Value $50 (395,597.4 shares)	$19,779,870.00	
"B" Preferred—$5 Dividend— No Par Value (803,375.1 shares)	17,203,610.07 (*)	
Common—No Par Value (6,580,375.1 shares)	15,679,296.30	
TOTAL CAPITAL STOCK		52,662,776.37
SURPLUS		29,690,244.32
TOTAL LIABILITIES AND CAPITAL		$158,679,883.60

(*) Subject to adjustment on final valuation of Victor Talking Machine Company net assets; Redemption Value $100 per share.

RADIO CORPORATION OF AMERICA AND SUBSIDIARY COMPANIES

CONSOLIDATED STATEMENT OF INCOME AND SURPLUS FOR THE YEAR ENDED DECEMBER 31, 1929

GROSS INCOME FROM ALL SOURCES		$182,137,738.65
LESS:		
Cost of Sales, General Operating, Development, Selling and Administrative Expenses, Interest and Depreciation		162,493,124.14
NET INCOME FOR THE YEAR (before Amortization of Patents, General Reserve and Federal Taxes)		$19,644,614.51
DEDUCT:		
Amortization of Patents	$ 909,052.60	
General Reserve	1,100,000.00	
Provision for Federal Taxes	1,743,000.00	
TOTAL DEDUCTIONS		3,752,052.60
NET INCOME FOR THE YEAR TRANSFERRED TO SURPLUS		$15,892,561.91
DIVIDENDS:		
On "A" Preferred	$1,373,775.46	
On "B" Preferred	3,037,500.00	
On Stocks of Victor Talking Machine Company (Prior to Conversion or Redemption)	1,094,434.05	
TOTAL DIVIDENDS		5,505,709.51
SURPLUS FOR THE YEAR		$10,386,852.40
SURPLUS AT DECEMBER 31, 1928		19,303,391.92
SURPLUS AT DECEMBER 31, 1929		$29,690,244.32

Radio Corporation's balance sheet showed it had $158.7 million in assets such as buildings, inventories, or patents, at the end of 1929. But the stock market valued the company at more than $1 billion during the fall.

WHAT IS A COMPANY WORTH?

Companies can be hard to value. But if a company has stock that is publicly traded, an investor can quickly figure out how much money the stock market thinks the company is worth at any given time. That worth, sometimes called "market capitalization" or "market value," reflects the current stock price multiplied by the total number of the company's shares. A company with 1 million shares outstanding and a stock that trades at $20 a share has a market value of $20 million.

Most of the time, a company's stock price reflects its profits, the growth of its business, and its future prospects. Investors tend to value fast-growing companies more highly than slowly growing companies.

Sometimes, though, investors get very excited about a company and bid the stock price up above what observers believe is logical. Sometimes investors lose faith in a company or its products and drive the stock down below what others believe it is worth. Over time, though, the push and pull between buyers and sellers results in a fair price.

pool and some of its individual members. Such sales were veiled attempts to make the stock active enough to capture the public's eye. But who was to say? The ticker was showing near-constant trading for Radio, and orders were coming in from all over the country.

For a few days, the pool bought a huge number of shares. *The Wall Street Journal* reported that it was the largest pool ever formed. The wealthy group was buying, the paper said, because it believed the company would be showing a big expansion of business and earnings. *The New York Times* saw a different motive. "Apparently the plan is to whip up the market," it said.

By then, the insiders' work was nearly done. The new shares had jumped to $109.25, up $35 in a week and a half. Based on those prices, the stock market was valuing Radio Corporation at more than $1 billion—impressive, considering the company had few hard assets and just $87 million in 1928 sales.

The peak would last only a short time. On Monday, March 18, the syndicate sold most of its Radio shares. Radio's price dropped sharply.

: -2.25...ATT: +.25...GM: +.25...Radio: -1.63...Steel: -.63...Dow: -2.25...ATT: +.25...GM: +.25...R

Within a week, the shares were back to $87.25. As usual, the pool members got out near the top. The little guys, who had dived in when the price was high, were left holding the stock.

In eight days of trading, the pool had bought and then sold nearly 1.5 million shares. Its members had made a profit of $5.6 million. Mrs. Sarnoff took home $58,342, making a little bundle from nothing. Mike Meehan made a killing too. He collected more than $850,000 in management fees and commissions from trading for the pool members. He couldn't join the pool—New York Stock Exchange rules prohibited that. So his wife joined and made a profit of $379,224. Billy Durant got his $400,000 back, plus $145,855. Altogether, they did quite well for about a week's work.

Except for a few references in stock-market columns, this run-up in Radio stock hardly got any attention at all. Newspapers had grown used to pools, quick price rallies, and equally impressive declines. Those were part of the modern stock-market game. But when all the details came out three years later in a Congressional hearing, Senator Carter Glass of Virginia had to wonder aloud about how fair and evenly matched this game was. Wasn't this just like playing poker with a man "at a card table with an extra card up his sleeve?" he asked.

For Mr. Durant, the pool's timing was just perfect. Within days, the Federal Reserve was clamping down on speculative lending, and the stock market went into a general swoon.

To Mr. Durant, the government men were scoundrels. The Federal Reserve was trying to keep the party from getting completely out of hand, but Mr. Durant thought the Fed was trying to ruin the party altogether. The government should just get out of the way, Mr. Durant believed, so he and the other speculators could continue to buy on the partial-payment plan and keep the market moving up.

To make his point, Mr. Durant hatched an audacious plan.

In late March 1929, Mr. Durant sent telegrams to one hundred top

Three Sides of Story!

SENATOR GLASS, of Virginia, says:

"William C. Durant is one of our great American financiers who have been luring amateur gamblers into Wall Street. Yes, and the President of the United States virtually jumped into the stock pit. High Government officials have deprecated any criticism of the stock market."

SENATOR COUZENS, of Michigan, says:

"Durant and other Wall Street financiers are seeking the repeal of the capital gain tax. When men like Durant find fault with whatever measures the Federal Reserve banks may take to suppress this orgy of speculation, it is perfectly obvious they are doing it for selfish reasons."

SENATOR GLASS.   SENATOR COUZENS,

W. C. DURANT.

William C. Durant Says:

"My compliments to Messrs. Glass and Couzens. Sarcastic and inaccurate statements by a few noisy United States Senators will not prevent the business men of America from protesting against the illegal action of the Federal Reserve Board.

"I have no ax to grind and no selfish motives in this fight for the strict observance of the present law or a new law that can be properly interpreted.

"With President Hoover I stand for law observance. Evi

Mr. Durant was never one to mince words. He willingly tangled with two U.S. Senators over whether the Federal Reserve should restrain lending and slow the flood of money pouring into stocks.

executives of industrial, utility, and railroad companies, asking a seemingly simple question: "Based on present conditions, prospects and plans for the future, do you think the present market price for (company name) is too high?"

Dozens of executives responded enthusiastically that their stock prices were just fine, given their prospects. Fred Wardel, president of Eureka Vacuum Cleaner Co., telegraphed back that no, his stock wasn't too high. But if the Fed continued to interfere with stock loans, he wrote, "we can all look for big drop in prices which will do great harm to present business." National Cash Register, Gillette Safety Razor, Chrysler Corporation, Kroger Grocery & Baking, and William Wrigley all resoundingly assured the auto man that their stocks were fairly priced.

Armed with support from national business leaders, Mr. Durant secretly took a train to Washington one April afternoon and arrived at the White House around 9:30 in the evening. President Hoover was having a dinner, and a secretary refused to summon him. But Mr. Durant, arriving unannounced, told the man who he was and insisted on delivering his important message directly and privately to the president.

Eventually, President Hoover saw him, Mr. Durant told reporters later. The bull of

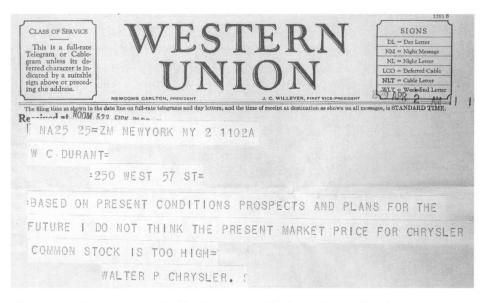

Received at ROOM 522 FICK BLDG.

NA25 25=ZM NEWYORK NY 2 1102A

W C DURANT=

:250 WEST 57 ST=

:BASED ON PRESENT CONDITIONS PROSPECTS AND PLANS FOR THE

FUTURE I DO NOT THINK THE PRESENT MARKET PRICE FOR CHRYSLER

COMMON STOCK IS TOO HIGH=

WALTER P CHRYSLER.

Many executives responded with telegrams to Mr. Durant's question, Is your stock price too high? Walter P. Chrysler agreed with Mr. Durant that stock prices were just fine, and the government didn't need to interfere.

the bulls warned the nation's leader that the government's actions threatened the financial stability of the country and that a financial disaster of unprecedented proportions could follow. "I told the president how I felt about the situation, and he listened with interest," Mr. Durant said. "I believed that I was doing a service to the country and to the President in telling him of what I believed was ahead."

Mr. Hoover may have listened—or the whole trip may have just been a concoction of Mr. Durant's arrogant imagination. Either way, the government did not budge. When stocks bounced around in late spring, Mr. Durant took some losses. No matter. "I'm the richest man in America," he said, pausing, "in friends."

By late October, he was still in the market, still looking for good buys. Like small investors, he owed some money to brokers, who would sell his stock as quickly as they would sell anyone else's. But as always, he believed the market would come back.

WESTERN UNION

Received at   1929 APR 2 PM 10 22

CFC1237 68 1 EXTRA NL=CH PINEHURST NCAR 2

W C DURANT=

    250 WEST 57 ST NEWYORK NY=   *KB*

YOUR WIRE ADDRESSED ME AT DETROIT FORWARDED TO ME HERE

STOP OUR BUSINESS SHOWS THE BEST PROSPECT IN THE HISTORY

OF OUR BUSINESS AND OUR STOCK WOULD NOT BE OUT OF LINE AT

QUITE AN ADVANCE OVER PRESENT QUOTED PRICE BUT BELIEVE IF

CONTINUED INTEREFERENCE WITH STOCK LOANS WE CAN ALL LOOK

FOR BIG DROP IN PRICES WHICH WILL DO GREAT HARM TO PRESENT

BUSINESS=

        EUREKA VACUUM CLEANER CO   FRED WARDEL PRESIDENT.

Mr. Durant sent one hundred such telegrams to well-known top executives in a creative effort to keep the stock market moving up and keep the government out of stock-market affairs.

After two calmer days, many Wall Street men might have agreed. Certainly, more shares would have to be sold on Monday to settle accounts. But *The New York Times* optimistically predicted "the hysteria of last Thursday had passed as quickly as it developed." *The Wall Street Journal* pointed out that the big banking group was still around to help out. "While the big banking interests stand behind the market there is no danger of a repetition of Thursday's break," it said.

Stock markets, they soon learned, are never so predictable.

W: -2.25...ATT: +.25...GM: +.25...RADIO: -1.63...STEEL: -.63...DOW: -2.25...ATT: +.25...GM:

OCTOBER

28

A BLOODY MONDAY

SINCE THURSDAY, OCTOBER 24, Richard Whitney, Thomas Lamont, and the bankers' group had been heroes, the men who boldly stepped up to combine their vast resources and stop the tremendous slide in prices. Their names and pictures had been on the front pages of the newspapers. To their embarrassment, people in the streets had applauded them as they arrived at work. Today, investors would be watching them closely again.

As the new week dawned, many people felt confident that the crisis had passed. Brokers had brought many of their books and records up to date for a fresh start. Wall Street was full of rumors that large investors would be scooping up bargains. But others, reflecting on last week's disaster, questioned that logic. This wasn't a little market anymore. How many more accounts would have to be sold because customers couldn't meet margin calls? Could the large investor be in any better shape than the small fry? And who would want to buy? After spending the weekend brooding over losses, wouldn't more stock owners want to join the mob getting out?

At his spot at Post 12 on the New York Stock Exchange floor, Mike Meehan was nervous. It was bad enough that Radio's stock was way down. But he was also worried about the general mood. The public seemed to be getting the notion that the banking group was going to try to make prices go up. He knew better. The bankers were only going to make sure there were buyers in the market, so the bottom wouldn't fall out. How would people react when it became clear that the bankers could only do so much?

It didn't take long to find out. Immediately after the opening gong, prices started to drop again. As on Thursday, the trading was fierce and downward. But this day had a different feel. Huge blocks of

RIGHT: On Monday a sparser crowd gathered in front of the New York Stock Exchange.

94

..DOW: -38.33...ATT: -34...GM: -6.75...RADIO: -18.38...STEEL: -17.50...DOW: -38.33...ATT: -

thousands of shares were changing hands, not little groups of one hundred or two hundred shares. While the small, lesser-known issues were particularly beat up last week, today the blue chips, the best of the best, were getting whacked. The stocks of U.S. Steel, American Telephone & Telegraph, and General Electric, the most seasoned of companies, tumbled. The little guys were wiped out the week before. Now, the big players were joining the panic. The decline was gathering steam.

The crowds at the customers' room were surprisingly thin. Customers who had given up on the market or been sold out stayed away—or maybe they went back to their jobs. Those who did visit sat

INSIDERS AND OUTSIDERS

No one knows a company better than its top managers. Executives such as the chairman of the board, the chief executive officer, and the president know a company intimately—where it does well and where it does poorly, what its sales and profits are in all its divisions, and how its competitors are faring. They are "insiders."

In the 1920s insiders could invest just like people outside the company. Using their vast inside information, they could buy or sell their company's stock whenever they wanted, and no one would find out. Executives could form private companies to invest in their company's stock without telling any other investors.

At the same time, companies didn't have to disclose a lot of details about their business. There were few rules governing exactly what facts investors needed to know. Investors were truly outsiders, with little access to important information about the companies behind their stocks.

That insiders could use their special knowledge in buying and selling their company's stock was another way that the 1920s stock market put little investors at a disadvantage.

paralyzed, eyes glued to the plunging numbers. They rarely spoke, and then only in whispers, with the hush of a graveyard.

By late morning, the New York Stock Exchange ticker was about a half hour behind in reporting prices. The price of Steel had sunk well below $200 a share, and other stocks were losing ground quickly. There were buyers, but prices often had to slide several dollars before they would come forward. Traders and investors alike strained for signs of support from investment trusts or the much-heralded banking group. But if either was truly buying, no one could tell.

The New York bankers watched the action closely. In

Albert H. Wiggin, the chairman of Chase National Bank, was one of the best-known bankers of the day. While trying to stabilize the market during the crash, he was also keeping a terrible secret.

addition to the silver-haired Mr. Lamont of J. P. Morgan, the group included some of the pillars of American business. Albert H. Wiggin, the serious-minded chairman of Chase National Bank, had been called "the most popular banker on Wall Street." Too poor to attend college, he had started as a bank clerk in Boston and worked his way up. An intense, somewhat humorless man with a temper like a firecracker, he had run Chase with an iron hand since 1911. Under his leadership, Chase had grown from a smallish bank to a major New York institution. At various times he also had been on the board of

Charles E. Mitchell was the chairman of National City Bank, one of the nation's biggest sellers of stocks to small-time investors.

directors of nearly sixty companies, helping govern some of the biggest corporations in America.

At sixty-one, Mr. Wiggin was eight years older than Charles E. Mitchell, the National City Bank chief who had thumbed his nose at the Washington establishment the preceding spring to keep the bull market roaring. Mr. Mitchell, a big, brawny man who walked several miles to work each day to get his exercise, was more outgoing than Mr. Wiggin and more influential.

In addition to running the largest bank in America, Mr. Mitchell paid close attention to the stock market. National City Bank had a sister company, called National City Company, that sold stocks and bonds to the public. In fact, it was the biggest in the nation, selling an average of $1.5 billion a year in securities "like so many pounds of coffee." Through hundreds of salesmen in more than fifty cities, it invested the savings of thousands of average Americans who thought they were dealing with a company that stood for safety, integrity, and business caution.

National City advertised its investment services in national magazines and pushed its salesmen to sell more through pep talks and sales contests. For years, it had sold only bonds, including the safe debts of the U.S. government and the sometimes not-so-safe-debts of countries like Germany, Greece, Peru, and Chile. As the public became enamored

Busy—*He takes a short-cut*

to sound investments

—so can you

In these "high pressure" days you must make every working minute count. Instead of shopping leisurely as you did a decade ago, you now save time by settling on one reliable house in each line—be it clothing, jewelry, furniture, or investments. The National City Company makes it easy for you to handle your investments on this time-and-worry-saving principle. It maintains offices in over fifty leading American cities for the convenience of busy men. Just telephone our office nearest you when you have funds to invest or wish market quotations or other investment information. Our experienced men will gladly help you.

The National City Company

National City Bank Building, New York

OFFICES IN 50 AMERICAN CITIES. INTERCONNECTED BY 11,000 MILES
OF PRIVATE WIRES. INTERNATIONAL BRANCHES AND CONNECTIONS.

National City Company was one of the most aggressive in wooing new investors to the stock market. In ads like this one, it promised to make investing easy and sound.

with stocks, National City began selling those in 1927, often peddling shares of companies in which it had a financial interest. In fact, its favorite stock to sell to the public was its own, National City Bank.

Mr. Mitchell had pulled National City Bank's stock off the New York Stock Exchange in early 1928, saying he was concerned about too much stock manipulation. At that time, the bank's stock was at $156, and it didn't trade very often or very heavily. Off the Exchange, the stock was traded "over the counter" between dealers making trades over the telephone. Since leaving the Big Board, the shares had climbed to a 1929 peak of $585, helped by the eager salesmen at National City Company. That year alone, National City Company had sold well over 1 million shares of the bank's stock to its customers.

Those stock and bond sales had made Mr. Mitchell very rich. The bank didn't tell its shareholders this, but it gave a portion of profits every year to its top executives. Mr. Mitchell made a modest salary of $25,000 a year, but he was taking home more than $1 million a year from the company's profits.

THE GOLD RUSH OF '29.

Small-time investors thought they were playing with the big boys as stock prices went up. But this New York *Telegram* cartoonist understood that when the market started falling, the little guys didn't stand a chance against the professionals.

As stock prices were plunging again that Monday, National City Bank's stock was as much on Mr. Mitchell's mind as the broader market. Bank stocks were being smashed, and National City's shares were down too. Just after 1 P.M., the big banker was seen at the Corner, entering the offices of J. P. Morgan. Just his presence started rumors that the bankers would be buying to help the market once again. For a brief time, prices steadied. Richard Whitney was buying on the exchange floor again too. But his small purchases hardly made a splash in the ocean of liquidation taking place around him.

Mr. Mitchell left Morgan smiling after half an hour. Most likely he had just arranged a large personal loan to try to prop up his own company's stock, but he wasn't saying. The market waited for a few minutes to see a reaction. There was none. The frenzy of the day's trading turned to hysteria. Terror took over. In the last hour of the trading day, nearly 3 million shares changed hands as prices swooned lower.

When the gong rang at 3 P.M., it sounded the end to the worst day ever in stock-market history. It took the ticker more than two and a half hours to finish delivering the full brunt of the bad news: On the New York Stock Exchange, an estimated $10 billion that investors had put into stocks had simply washed away in five hours. A good part of that loss was in the sixteen biggest and most popular stocks. U.S. Steel had fallen $17.50 a share to close at $186. Richard Whitney's Thursday bid at $205 seemed like ancient history.

In one day, General Electric lost $47.50 to $250 a share; Radio slid $18.38 to $40.25; and AT&T was down $34 to $232. In all, 9.2 million shares changed hands. The Dow Jones Industrial Average of thirty stocks lost 38.33 points, a devastating decline of 12.8 percent that is still the second-largest in stock-market history. It would be more than half a century before the average would see a one-day percentage drop like that again.

The speed and depth of the disaster caught many by surprise.

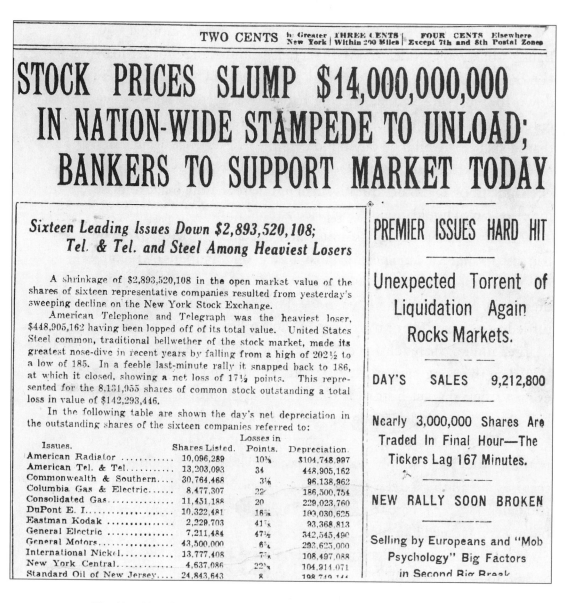

STOCK PRICES SLUMP $14,000,000,000 IN NATION-WIDE STAMPEDE TO UNLOAD; BANKERS TO SUPPORT MARKET TODAY

Sixteen Leading Issues Down $2,893,520,108; Tel. & Tel. and Steel Among Heaviest Losers

A shrinkage of $2,893,520,108 in the open market value of the shares of sixteen representative companies resulted from yesterday's sweeping decline on the New York Stock Exchange.

American Telephone and Telegraph was the heaviest loser, $448,905,162 having been lopped off of its total value. United States Steel common, traditional bellwether of the stock market, made its greatest nose-dive in recent years by falling from a high of 202½ to a low of 185. In a feeble last-minute rally it snapped back to 186, at which it closed, showing a net loss of 17½ points. This represented for the 8,131,955 shares of common stock outstanding a total loss in value of $142,293,446.

In the following table are shown the day's net depreciation in the outstanding shares of the sixteen companies referred to:

Issues.	Shares Listed.	Losses in Points.	Depreciation.
American Radiator	10,096,289	10⅜	$104,748,997
American Tel. & Tel...........	13,203,093	34	448,905,162
Commonwealth & Southern.....	30,764,468	3⅛	96,138,962
Columbia Gas & Electric......	8,477,307	22	186,500,754
Consolidated Gas...............	11,451,188	20	229,023,760
DuPont E. I....................	10,322,481	16⅜	169,030,625
Eastman Kodak	2,229,703	41⅞	93,368,813
General Electric	7,211,484	47½	342,545,490
General Motors.................	43,500,000	6¾	293,625,000
International Nickel...........	13,777,408	7⅞	108,497,088
New York Central.............	4,637,086	22⅛	104,914,071
Standard Oil of New Jersey....	24,843,643	8	198,749,144

PREMIER ISSUES HARD HIT

Unexpected Torrent of Liquidation Again Rocks Markets.

DAY'S SALES 9,212,800

Nearly 3,000,000 Shares Are Traded In Final Hour—The Tickers Lag 167 Minutes.

NEW RALLY SOON BROKEN

Selling by Europeans and "Mob Psychology" Big Factors in Second Big Break.

The New York Times headline on Tuesday captured the huge drop in stock prices on Monday, October 28—and the optimism that bankers could stop the fall.

...Dow: -38.33...ATT: -34...GM: -6.75...Radio: -18.38...Steel: -17.50...Dow: -38.33...ATT: -34...G

President Hoover and his cabinet, while believing that stocks had been too high, now fretted that the reaction was too severe. They worried that stock problems would spoil the country's long prosperity. But, they reassured themselves and others, business really was strong and should withstand the market's problems.

Once again, businessmen tried to soothe the public's fraying faith. Mr. Wiggin of Chase National Bank proclaimed the decline was "the natural fruit of the orgy of speculation." But, he offered, "None of the corporations or institutions I am connected with is selling stocks at this time. We are, rather, buying. I am convinced genuine bargains are available at this moment."

True, as at National City, some people at Chase National were buying Chase stock, trying to prop up the price. But Mr. Wiggin's proclamation about his confidence in the markets concealed a terrible lie. Through a private company he owned, *he* was selling. And he wasn't just selling any old stock any old way. Since September he had been selling thousands of Chase National shares short, betting that his own company's stock would go down. The previous Friday, in fact, his private company had borrowed five hundred more Chase National shares and sold them, intending to pay them back later. The coach was secretly betting against his own team.

Later, he would say that he thought "prices of bank stocks were ridiculous" and he believed his family ought to reduce its Chase holdings while the price was high. During September and October his private company had borrowed more than $10 million' worth of Chase shares from others and sold them. In December, those same shares would be bought back for about $6 million, purchased with money borrowed from Chase National itself. During the greatest stock-market decline of all time, Mr. Wiggin would make a personal profit of $4 million.

No one, not the public or the other members of the banking

group, had a clue about those personal dealings. When Mr. Wiggin gathered with Mr. Mitchell, Mr. Lamont, and the other bankers after the market closed to review their strategy, their focus was on how to stop the devastation. The group met from late afternoon until nearly 7 P.M., agreeing that they would provide support where there was none. But they were powerless to turn the entire market.

In talking with reporters afterward, Mr. Lamont again tried to be reassuring. He repeated that the banking group would buy stocks to keep the market orderly, though it couldn't prevent a decline in prices. But privately, bankers were telling newsmen to be optimistic. The tide should turn tomorrow, they said, and buying should be heavy. Bankers, investment trusts, and others with deep pockets should be snapping up bargains. The newspaper headlines were full of hope. "Giant Bank Pool Pledged to Avert Disaster," read one. And another: "Bankers to Support Market Today." But could any group, no matter how powerful or how rich, really stop an avalanche?

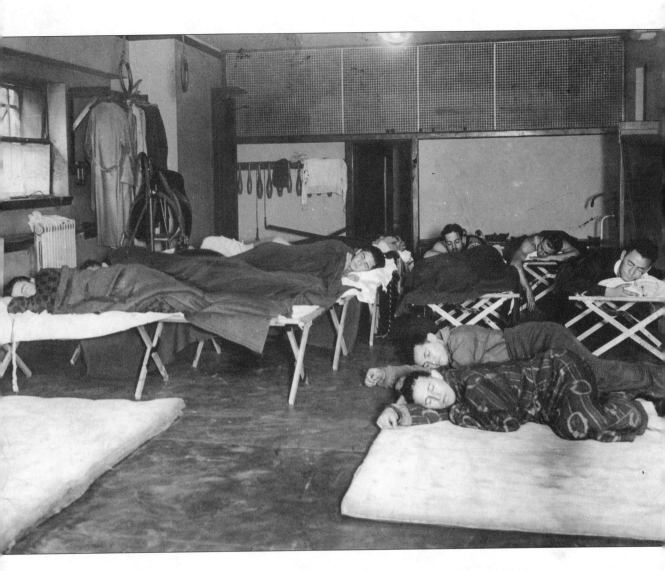

A gymnasium in the financial district
set up cots for tired workers to catch
a little sleep after working late into
the night.

A BLOODY MONDAY

OCTOBER

29

BLACK TUESDAY

AFTER THE DAMAGE of October 28, the men on the Stock Exchange floor couldn't help feeling jittery. It would be another frantic day, to be sure, and they would be in the spotlight. This morning at Post 12, Mike Meehan was dressed better than usual. He was wearing his blue suit, his shoes were shined, and a pearl pin held his tie in place. He looked something like a man on his way to a funeral.

Overnight, orders to sell thousands and thousands of shares of Radio had come in. Mr. Meehan tried to encourage his staff, to relax them. He told jokes. He traded gossip. Though the stocks he owned personally were way down, hurting his personal wealth, he knew his specialist firm would be making money as long as people kept trading.

Even before the market opened, the New York Stock Exchange was harried. Discarded pieces of paper already littered the floor. Crowds jostled around the trading posts as clerks and traders ran wildly around the perimeter. Mr. Meehan's staff braced itself for the opening, feeling what it "must have been like for the defenders of the Alamo as they waited to be overrun."

The attack started with the first vibration of the gong. The cries of *"Sell! Sell! Sell!"* drowned out the opening sound. In the first few minutes, more than six hundred thousand shares of U.S. Steel, the stock that had been the pride and hope of the bulls, were sold. The price dipped. Men shoved, swore at, and clawed at the stock specialist, desperate to dump the stock. For a brief moment, enough buyers emerged to move the price up slightly. But it quickly sank back again.

Radio shares dropped more than $10 a share to $30. At Post 6, two clerks trying to sell a stock got into a fistfight. The specialist for General Electric separated them, and quickly returned to his job trying to find buyers for all the sellers. At Post 8, shares of Montgomery Ward were "falling quicker than cans off a supermarket shelf."

Stocks were being thrown on the market in huge blocks of five thousand, ten thousand, and fifty thousand shares. As brokers pushed

and shoved to sell, specialists tried to delay trades while they searched for buyers. A few clever folks found bargains. On Monday, White Sewing Machine Company slid to $11.13 from a year-high of $48. On Tuesday, someone—rumored to be a quick-thinking messenger—put in a bid for

Worried about what was left of their investments, thousands of people stood outside the New York Stock Exchange to find out what was happening on one of the busiest, and darkest, trading days ever.

$1 a share. In the absence of other buyers, he actually got the stock, allowing him to turn a considerable profit later.

As prices fell faster and faster, people came unglued. A middle-aged man with a tear in his jacket broke out from the crowd, moaning, "I'm sold out! Sold out!" Another man, screaming at the top of his lungs that he had been ruined, grabbed a messenger by the hair and lifted the youngster off his feet. The messenger twisted and screamed, but the man wouldn't let him go. Finally, the youngster broke free and fled the Exchange crying, leaving the yelling man with a fist full of hair.

One broker fell to the floor and began to crawl about wildly. A nurse who hurried to help him heard the man spouting gibberish and thought he had gone mad. In fact, he had only lost his false teeth while shouting an order, and had nearly been trampled trying to find them.

Just thirty minutes into the trading day, more than 3 million shares already had traded, and stock values had fallen by more than $2 billion.

Once again, thousands of people began to gather at the Corner, outside the Stock Exchange and across from J. P. Morgan. The excitement of last week was gone, replaced by a mood as gray as the chilly October day. The unsettling thrill of the unknown had turned to fear and then horror as the unimaginable continued to play out in front of them. Professionals and amateurs alike visited Trinity Church down the street to pray, filling the midday service and the chapel all day.

Safe-deposit companies, where residents could store their valuables in secure vaults, said two to three times more visitors than usual came to remove stock certificates or jewels and other valuables from their safes. Savings banks were crowded with people seeking to withdraw cash, and insurance companies were swamped with customers wanting to cash out their insurance policies.

Across New York City, pawn shops were overrun with men and women looking to swap their most valuable possessions for a cash loan. One woman pawned her $5,000 mink coat for a $300 loan to meet a margin call. She wouldn't get her coat back unless she could repay the loan with interest. The pawn shops, considered the lender of last resort, said they turned away hundreds of people because they didn't have enough cash to make loans on all the jewels that were offered.

At the brokerage houses, tense and emotional customers once again jammed in to watch the prices. The ticker was running behind yet again, so much so, that some houses simply let the tape run out. Instead, brokers relied on phone calls from the Stock Exchange's quotation department and a few updates from the Dow Jones News Service. When prices fell, the brokers didn't wait long for customers to come in with cash to meet margin calls. They made one

How steep was the stock market decline? Take a look at the Dow Jones Industrial Average for October 1929.

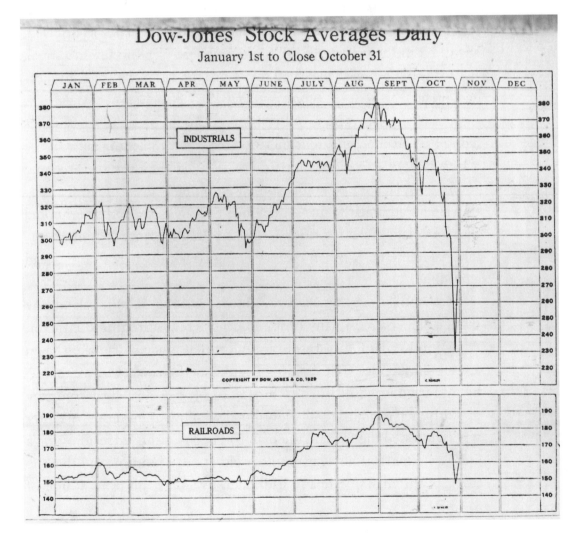

Dow-Jones Stock Averages Daily
January 1st to Close October 31

COPYRIGHT BY DOW JONES & CO. 1929

INDUSTRIALS

RAILROADS

call, and if there wasn't an answer, the stocks were sold. In a market where millions of dollars were dissolving by the minute, there was no time to wait.

The week before, brokerage houses complained that women had been hysterical and temperamental about the downturn. But today their mood was more resigned. Gray-haired women, some wealthy widows and others former schoolteachers relying on their investments for retirement, sat in customers' rooms, talking quietly or not at all. "There goes our trip to Europe," moaned one. Another woman was said to have lost $800,000. But, said the *New York Telegram,* "if she cried, she did it in the privacy of her boudoir. There were no tears to streak her make-up when she learned the last of the sad news at her brokerage office."

In one special women-only customers' room near the fancy stores along Park Avenue, an attendant stood ready with smelling salts, in case a lady fainted. He didn't need them, nor did they use the "retiring room"—a place set aside for women who might need medical attention after watching the market's plunge. Still, *The New York Times* noted that some ladies seemed ready to give up "high finance" for more traditional interests. "Women Traders Going Back to Bridge Games," read a headline.

Men took the news hard too. In Providence, Rhode Island, the owner of a coal company dropped dead while watching the ticker. A man in Kansas City, Missouri, shot himself twice in the chest in an attempted suicide. "Tell the boys I can't pay them what I owe them," he told friends who rushed to his aid. In New York, a cigar company executive fell from his tenth-floor hotel window to his death. A waiter who witnessed the fall said the man had been on the ledge adjusting a radio antenna. But news accounts couldn't resist pointing out that the stock of the man's company had fallen to $4 a share from a high of $113.50.

Winston Churchill, spending his last day in America before sailing home to England, claimed that a man in his hotel fell fifteen stories. The man "was dashed to pieces, causing a wild commotion and the arrival of the fire brigade," he wrote. "Quite a number of persons seem to have overbalanced themselves by accident in the same sort of way." Rumors of devastated speculators leaping from windows spread again, but nearly all of them turned out to be false.

What was true was that people from all over the Western world were selling. The volume of transatlantic telephone calls was double the normal rate. Telephone lines were clogged between New York and the Midwest and between New York and California. Western Union was sending two to three times more messages than usual, and cable operators from Europe reported a heavy flow of messages headed to the financial district.

From seemingly everywhere, the message was *Sell! Sell! Sell!* At the New York Stock Exchange, any slight rallies were brief. The big banking group may have been buying, but too many people were selling too many shares for them to make much difference. Trying to support the market was "like trying to stem the falls of Niagara."

Even after the trauma of the last few days, this collapse was so complete, it was astounding. "The liquidation in the stock market was on so vast a scale as to parallel a war calamity," said Richard Whitney, the Morgan broker and vice president of the Stock Exchange. Stock exchanges in London, Chicago, San Francisco, Boston, and Montreal were following the New York Exchange down. Observers couldn't help but feel they were witnessing a once-in-a-lifetime financial catastrophe. Never had so many people lost so much money so quickly.

The governors of the New York Stock Exchange were in the madness on the floor, looking for ways to use their own wealth to stem the selling torrent. But it was no use. Mr. Whitney called an emergency meeting at noon to consider closing the Stock Exchange. By then,

113

Amid the rage for stocks, an unusual breed of company became fashionable. Investment companies were created solely to buy stocks of other companies. The idea was that professionals would make better stock picks than little investors would. Little investors just had to buy the stock of an investment trust, and their money would be wisely invested for them.

All kinds of investment companies and trusts sold shares to the public. But once they had cash in hand, many of the investment trusts didn't use the money very wisely.

Many trusts borrowed heavily, adding to their costs and their risks. Others bought stocks that no one else would buy, even if the companies behind them were worthless. Some trusts used shareholder money to buy stock in other investment companies, creating a pyramid of sorts. They paid big fees to their managers. They didn't allow shareholders to have any say. And perhaps worst of all, they never disclosed the stocks they actually owned, so shareholders really didn't know what they had invested in.

Even so, Wall Street provided and the public bought. In 1929, a new trust was created almost every day, raising about $3 billion of investor money. Little investors bid up the prices of these companies well above what their assets were worth.

When the air began to come out of the stock market, the stock prices of investment companies and trusts fell hard and fast. Managers tried to stop the declines by buying their own stocks. But they were only throwing good money after bad. "Men have been swindled by other men on many occasions," wrote economist John Kenneth Galbraith. "But autumn of 1929 was, perhaps, the first occasion when men succeeded on a large scale in swindling themselves."

8 million shares had been traded, nearly as many as on Thursday, and the trading day had three more hours to go. Rather than raise alarm by meeting in the usual Governing Committee Room, Mr. Whitney asked the Stock Exchange elite to meet in a basement office. The forty

governors wandered downstairs in twos and threes, trying not to attract attention.

As the powers of the New York Stock Exchange met, the panic continued to rage. Thousands of people thundering in the melee overhead created a constant din. Since the office was small, governors were forced to stand or sit on tables. "Every few minutes the latest prices were announced, with quotations moving swiftly and irresistibly downwards. The feeling of those present was revealed by their habit of continually lighting cigarettes, taking a puff or two, putting them out and lighting new ones—a practice which soon made the narrow room blue with smoke and extremely stuffy," Mr. Whitney recalled.

Some governors feared the Stock Exchange would collapse. The system had not been designed for such immense trading. The late ticker meant traders and speculators did not know current prices, adding to their fright. Telephone lines to brokers' offices were congested. There were so many orders that the usual wooden boxes were full and clerks were stashing the overflow in large trash baskets. As they frantically made trades, the specialists didn't always get the names of all the buyers and sellers. The mechanics were so limited that keeping up with the enormous volume of the last few days was, Mr. Whitney said, "as though one should try to force a gallon of water into a quart bottle."

But the bankers and other governors found the notion of closing the Stock Exchange "unthinkable." People were scared enough already. A closing might also create an impromptu market on the sidewalks that was even more uncertain and volatile that the wild one upstairs. In addition, the bankers knew that loan money for stocks was drying up. Companies and out-of-town banks, which had lent so many millions of dollars in recent months so speculators could buy on margin, were taking their money back. The New York banks were quietly stepping up to help, making new loans to take the place of the old ones. They were staying open into the evening and even lowering

To get the latest stock prices, brokerage firms could call the clerks at the New York Stock Exchange's quotation department. But even they were overwhelmed on October 29.

.....Dow: -30.57...ATT: -28...GM: -7.50...Radio: -1.75...Steel: -12...Dow: -30.57...ATT: -28...GM:

margin requirements to ease the panic. But they were in a risky situation. If the Stock Exchange closed and they could not sell the stocks that backed those loans, banks could fail.

The governors agreed that the Stock Exchange should stay open. But they also agreed to meet again that evening to reconsider. As the men filed out the door to return to the grim reality upstairs, Mr. Whitney had a reminder. Appearances were important. "Now get your smiles on, boys!" he urged them.

The trading floor was a depressing sight. Men stood in discarded paper up to their ankles, and the selling continued. By 1:30 P.M., trading volume had passed 12 million shares. With both confidence and values disappearing, there seemed to be no bottom, no end to the crisis.

Then, in late afternoon, a little bit of upbeat news clacked across the Dow Jones News Service. American Can declared a special $1-a-share payment to its shareholders, and raised its regular dividend, too. U.S. Steel, after reviewing its performance for the first nine months of the year, also said it would make a special payment of $1 a share to its shareholders. American business was reminding Wall Street that the problems were with stocks, not with factories and products.

Maybe it was that news. Maybe the banking group was finally making a difference. Or maybe the storm had simply spun itself out for the time being. Some stocks started to turn. Gradually, the mood on the exchange began to shift. One more wave of selling would wash over the floor before the final gong rang. But the traders and specialists, brokers and clerks also felt a change. A floor had been found. Now the market could rebound.

The rout had been thorough and painful. More than 16.4 million shares changed hands, far and above the trading volume ever imagined. That, however, didn't include trades of less than 100 shares and trades that didn't go out on the ticker. Including those, probably 23 million shares were traded. The New York Stock Exchange figured that its thousands of tickers nationwide had spit out some fifteen thousand miles of ticker tape recording all those sales.

The day's final loss was awful, but it would have been worse without the late turnaround. Another $8 billion to $9 billion in stock values vanished on the New York Stock Exchange, and billions more disappeared on the New York Curb Exchange and others. Thanks to the late rally, the Dow Jones Industrial Average slid slightly less than on Monday, by 30.57 points, or nearly 12 percent.

In just six days of trading, the Dow Jones Industrial Average had fallen by a third. More than $25 billion in individual wealth was lost. Some people would never recover.

The devastation left a huge mess, and cleaning it up would take some time. But the Stock Exchange governors decided that the market should stay open to keep confidence up. Brokerage houses, specialists, and banks would have piles of paperwork to take care of. There were many unpleasant surprises: incomplete records, margin accounts that had been sold out twice, and work missed in the rush of trading. One worn-out clerk on the Stock Exchange floor found an entire wastebasket full of orders that he had stuck in a corner for safekeeping. The trades had never been made.

Mike Meehan tried to remain upbeat. His staff was working around the clock to stay on top of the trading. He personally had suffered big losses, but he knew he needed his people to keep his company going. That day, he walked into his office after the market closed and called the office manager. "I understand I'm broke," he told his manager. "Guess we'd better give all the boys in the office a two weeks' bonus to prove it."

In Washington, the Federal Reserve Board met all day but declined to offer any comment. Assistant U.S. Secretary of Commerce Julius Klein went on national radio to repeat that America's industrial and

The Trader's Lament
(After Tuesday)

Who cares what stocks may do today?
My hair has long since turned to gray.
Dow-Jones flashed prices from the floor
While brokers called for margin: "More!"

They'd said: "Your list is long and wide
And also well diversified."
Later: "Margin! Send it quick!
Your holdings look a little sick."

O, boil me well in Standard Oil!
I'd slipped from Anaconda's coil
When Purity touched fifty-five,—
Down forty-four—O, Man Alive!

I wriggled like a frightened eel!
From out the avalanche of Steel
"Margin!" "Hold on, I'm nearly broke,
Sell Pennsylvania Coal & Coke."

They'd sold my Motors, sold my Copper,
When Adolf Gobel came a cropper,
They backed me up against the wall
And pickled me in Alcohol.

This can't go on," somebody said,
"The crash will make the bulls see red.
Look, Curtis Pub is sitting tight;
The question is, is Curtiss-Wright?"

Farewell to old A.T. & T.
And all I owned from A to Z
Had vanished like the morning dew,
(They had to take my I.O.U.)

I'm sick and tired of raids and marches;
I've nothing now but fallen arches
Alas, that this should come to pass,—
Garcon, turn on that Brooklyn Gas!

commercial structure was sound. Business leaders insisted that the stock market's woes were masking the fine year they were having.

Some took a further step to soften worries. Julius Rosenwald, chairman of Sears, Roebuck and Company, promised to provide money to protect the margin accounts of any of Sears's forty thousand employees. New York City Mayor Jimmy Walker urged motion picture exhibitors to avoid showing unpleasant newsreels about the stock market that would hurt the public morale. Give viewers "a chance to forget their financial losses on the stock market and look with hope to the future," the mayor urged them.

Even some newspapers tried to sugarcoat the day's events, or find

A *Wall Street Journal* writer took a tongue-in-cheek approach to coping with the loss of so much money.

Most newspapers were somber about the stock market crash. But not the entertainment publication *Variety.*

some humor in it. "Stocks Steady After Decline," read the headline in *The Wall Street Journal. Variety,* the entertainment newspaper, was cheeky: "Wall St. Lays an Egg." The *New York Daily News* inserted cartoons amid its account of the stock-market wreckage. "I got diabetes at 42," said one little cartoon man to another. "That's nothing," the other man replied. "I got Radio at 93."

But no matter how happy the movies were or how funny the cartoons, many would find it hard to cheer up. So much had been lost in the last six days. Billions and billions of dollars were gone, and dissolving with them were the dreams and hopes and plans of many. "The tragic story of Tuesday, Oct. 29, 1929, will not be written," said the *New York Daily News,* "until the record is compiled of homes which must be mortgaged, lifetime

RIGHT: Lights burned late into the night on October 29 as Wall Street tried to sort out the devastation from the day's decline.

.Radio: -1.75...Steel: -12...Dow: -30.57...ATT: -28...GM:-7.50...   BLACK TUESDAY

savings which have vanished and the thousands of men and women who had retired after years of toil and saving go out seeking employment to sustain them for their remaining years, which they thought had been taken care of by investments considered prudent."

The big guys had drawn the little guys into the boom with the lure of guiding them, of sharing a piece of 1920s prosperity. As more and more little players rolled in, the big players saw great wealth and power within their reach, and couldn't resist stretching for even more. It had been a fun ride. But now the game was over for all of them.

OCTOBER

30

AFTERMATH

WEDNESDAY, OCTOBER 30, 1929, was a nasty, drizzly day in New York City. But for the first time in a dark week, Wall Street managed to find something to smile about.

Buoyed by optimistic bargain-hunters, stocks climbed from the opening gong. Orders came in from all over: Foreign buyers returned. Speculators whose accounts were still intact couldn't resist gambling again now that their favorite stocks were low. A broker could be heard shouting into a telephone to a client, "It's the chance of a lifetime! You'll never get a chance like this again in your life! If you've got money to buy, buy everything!"

Even working men and women with just $500 or $1,000 to spare showed up at brokers' offices, begging to buy. They knew that many, many people had been wiped out. But this was their chance, they believed, to finally get in on the stock bonanza.

On the floor of the New York Stock Exchange, traders and brokers cheered when they saw the opening numbers rise. Trading once again was extremely heavy, but the job was easier when the news was good.

There was more good news to come. The officials of the Stock Exchange were recognizing that the fatigue and exhaustion of all of Wall Street's workers was taking a huge toll. Brokers, clerks, messengers, and bank employees had worked through the last two nights trying to stay on top of the immense paperwork created by the enormous trading. Some workers had not been home in a week and had grabbed what sleep they could get in chairs or on office couches. Half-eaten sandwiches and empty coffee cups littered their desks.

On the main banking floor of the National City Bank on Wall Street, weary messengers formed long lines in front of the loan windows, waiting to deliver bundles of stock certificates that backed loans. Unable to stand any longer, many curled up on the marble floor and fell asleep. Charles Mitchell, passing through, saw the sleeping boys and ordered security guards to bring chairs for all of them.

John D. Rockefeller was ninety years old at the time of the crash, but still alert enough to tell the public that he was now buying stocks. His comments cheered investors.

This time, when the governors discussed whether to close the Exchange, the answer was clear. "It was not an economic problem—it was a human problem," said Richard Whitney. Normally, the Stock Exchange would shorten a trading day by opening on time and ending early, so there would be more time in the afternoon to settle transactions. "But what Wall Street needed was, after all, sleep," Mr. Whitney recalled. So the Stock Exchange opened trading two hours late on Thursday, October 31, and closed on Friday, November 1, and Saturday, November 2, to give workers a much-needed chance to rest and to catch up.

As acting president, Mr. Whitney would need to tell the people on the trading floor of the scheduled closing. Ordinarily, the tickers would be stopped for an announcement. But he didn't want any disruptions. Instead, the tickers kept clacking as he delivered the news, which, he said, "came as a great relief to all, and to our satisfaction was greeted with loud cheers."

A little later, Wall Street would have one more chance to cheer. In the afternoon, the secretive and stoic oilman John D. Rockefeller, at ninety years old one of America's richest men, broke his usual silence. In a statement that quickly crossed news tickers, he said he supported the stock market. "Believing that the fundamental conditions of the country are sound and that there is nothing in the business situation to warrant the destruction of values that has taken place on the exchanges during the past week, my son and I have for some days been purchasing sound common stocks," he said. The pair would continue purchasing "in substantial amounts at levels which we believe represent sound investment values."

The public couldn't help but be buoyed by the confidence of such a powerful and influential man—though comedian and singer Eddie Cantor had a different view. Sure, the Rockefellers were buying, Mr. Cantor said later. "Who else had any money left?"

Lifted by the distinct change in mood, some stocks jumped by $10 to $30 a share as more than 10.7 million shares were traded. The Dow Jones Industrial Average finished the day up 28.40 points, or 12.3 percent, making up a good bit of Tuesday's losses. (The gain to this day is the second-biggest percentage jump in stock-market history.)

On Thursday, Henry Ford announced that he was cutting car prices by $15 to $45 a model to make them more affordable. The price on a Ford coupe dropped $35, to $490. Trading on this day was heavy too, though it was a shortened session.

The Stock Exchange then closed for three days, though it was difficult to tell it was shut down. Wall Streeters slept hard and worked hard. The trading floor was open, telephones rang, the annunciator board banged and rattled, and men like Mike Meehan stood at their posts to untangle dozens of twisted transactions.

Because of the heavy trading volume, the Stock Exchange decided to reduce trading hours through much of November and close on Saturdays. On Monday, November 4, when the market reopened, stocks fell again. The Stock Exchange was closed Tuesday for a local Election Day. Prices rallied somewhat on Thursday and Friday. But the following week, another wave of selling blew through.

Monday, November 11, started out relatively calm, with trading slow compared with that of the previous few weeks. But in the late morning, selling grew brisk and prices fell sharply once again.

That night, the banking group, which had grown to include a number of top New York banks, got together in a long evening meeting. In just a few weeks, said Edward M. Lamont, Thomas Lamont's grandson and biographer, the banker's group had spent $137.8 million to buy 1.4 million shares to keep the market moving during its neediest days. As they reviewed their work, the group decided that the market seemed stable enough to hold its own. The bankers agreed to stop buying stocks—but they did not tell the public. The same day, Thomas Lamont was featured on the cover of *Time* magazine, which recognized his leadership during the crisis.

On Tuesday, stocks slid sharply as volume picked up again. This time, the bankers weren't around to buy. Another group of small speculators, who had managed to hold on this far, saw their luck

FIFTEEN CENTS   November 11, 1929

TIME
The Weekly Newsmagazine

Volume XIV   THOMAS WILLIAM LAMONT   Number 20
He felt the helm respond.
(See Domestic)

Thomas W. Lamont made the cover of *Time* magazine for organizing the banking group that had tried to stop the stock market's fall.

finally run out. Remember the anonymous auto salesman who had sold his car dealership to trade in stocks? As his stock riches had multiplied, he had bought a fashionable New York City apartment and enrolled his son in an exclusive private school. In late October, he watched brokers tell one client after another that he had been sold out. "I saw men's hair literally turn white. I saw a woman faint dead away; they carried her out cold. I heard a middle-aged doctor say, 'There goes my son's college education.' Terrible sights. Terrible sounds," the salesman recalled. But he was still in good shape. He congratulated himself on his conservative investing.

Then on Monday, November 11, his broker tapped him on the shoulder and called him into a private office. The time had come for the salesman to "strengthen his account" with more cash. Prices were so low that his stocks were no longer secure. The salesman withdrew his $70,000 in winnings, his entire bank account, and turned it over to the broker. But prices sank again, and it wasn't enough. On Tuesday, November 12, all of his stocks were sold. In his push to earn more, he had lost it all. "I should have been perfectly satisfied. I should have said, 'It's enough for any man,'" he said. When he had built $4,000 in savings into nearly $300,000, "I was miserable because it wasn't half a million. And if it had become half a million, I should have wanted a million. Greed—it's the most insidious disease of all." Within weeks, the salesman sold his apartment, moved to the country, and went back to work, selling cars just as when he had started out.

On Wednesday, November 13, one final flood of selling washed through the market. The Dow Jones Industrial Average finished at 198.69, wiping out nearly all of the gains since the first of 1928. Since the peak in early September, the average of thirty key stocks had fallen almost in half.

Every day, it seemed, the newspapers reported on the suicide of another prominent man who took his own life after suffering financial losses. The president of County Trust Company shot himself. The president of Rochester Gas and Electric died after intentionally opening the gas jets in his home. He had lost more than $1 million in the crash. The headlines were dramatic, but the real numbers were less so, found John Kenneth Galbraith, an economist who examined the stock-market crash. Suicides per one hundred thousand people in New York City and the nation rose only slightly during 1929, and the number of self-inflicted deaths was actually higher in the summer, when the market was soaring, than in the months during and after the crash.

Many speculators, injured but not destroyed, had to change their lifestyles, selling expensive homes or giving up regular pleasures. Even Mike Meehan had to cut back. He asked his wife to fire the household help. But to keep appearances up and maintain his reputation, he kept his car and driver. Once again, Elizabeth Meehan had to use her skills in scraping by.

Almost immediately, the nation felt an impact. Loans for stock purchases disappeared almost overnight, shrinking an incredible $4 billion in two months.

Slowly, the number of unemployed workers, already relatively high, started to rise as clerks, landscapers, housekeepers, and others lost their jobs. Anxious and confused, consumers cut back. Auto sales, department stores sales, and even radio sales fell. Still, as deep as losses were, hardly anyone saw them as making a permanent dent in American prosperity. Times were too good, business was too strong.

Amid a college football scandal involving payments to Ivy League players and other headlines, the problems of the stock market became routine news. In late November, Commander Richard E. Byrd and companions made the first flight over the South Pole, sharing their experience in newspaper journals. *The New York Times,* which had helped sponsor the flight, declared the accomplishment the biggest news story of 1929.

Many jobs were lost as the economy became weaker. Some men turned to selling apples on the street to get by.

E.H.H. Simmons, the president of the New York Stock Exchange, returned from his long honeymoon in Hawaii in December, after all the market damage had been done. He saw the crash as simply a sign of excess. The market had gotten ahead of itself as so many companies sold shares and stock prices rose. "In my own judgment," he wrote in his president's report for 1929-30, "the panicky atmosphere which arose in October and November was largely due to 'security indigestion' brought about by this colossal issuance of new share offerings."

In fact, starting in January 1930, stock prices started to pick up again, and trading volume got frisky. Small speculators slowly returned, hoping that they could catch the next spike that was certain to happen. From January to April 1930, the Dow Jones Industrial Average climbed, regaining about half of the losses it suffered in October and November.

In April, Mr. Simmons decided to retire, and the New York Stock Exchange named Richard Whitney, the October hero, as its new president. The Exchange directors also presented Mr. Whitney with a special memento of his famous bid for U.S. Steel shares: the old Post 2, one of the tall, street lamp–like trading posts that had been on the Stock Exchange floor before the huge new U-shaped posts were installed. He proudly displayed the post in the lobby of his office.

Not long after, the market began to turn down again. Speculators refused to give up. The number of shareholders, of people investing their savings, continued to grow. Each hoped for another spectacular rebound. This time, though, there were no banking groups, no big investors, and no pools that could really make a difference. Something else was happening in the American economy, and stock prices were reflecting the change.

Perhaps the biggest myth about the stock-market crash of 1929 is that it started the Great Depression. Economists and historians insist that it did not. What it did do was slash the wealth of the richest. In the late 1920s the wealthy were relatively small in number, yet they bought most of the luxury items and other consumer goods that had kept the economy humming. When their spending slowed, many felt it. The crash also changed the public's attitude from optimism to caution. "In 1929 our guide was greed," said Otto H. Kahn, a prominent New York investment banker. "At the end of 1929 our guide was fear. I think they are the two worse guides in the world, greed and fear."

But even fear, powerful as it is, can't change a country's direction alone. The stock-market crash was like a single large rock toppling down a mountainside. By itself, it was not a landslide.

The crash might have been only another stock-market correction, a blip on the national economic radar, if the country had not had many other problems that the stock-market surge had masked. Despite the insistence of businessmen, business wasn't all that sound. In fact, an economic contraction, or recession, had started that summer, when auto sales, home construction, and steel production had dropped off. The banking system was wobbly and troubled. Hundreds of banks closed their doors during the late 1920s, and many more would close during the 1930s. When savings could disappear just as easily in a bank as in the stock market, no place seemed safe for hard-earned money. On top of that, serious political problems in Europe rippled over the ocean into U.S. business.

Policy decisions by President Hoover and his advisers seemed only to make matters worse. A tax cut had little effect because most Americans paid very little in taxes. As businesses ran into more trouble and put more workers out of jobs, the government did little to help the growing numbers of unemployed. In 1929, about 4 million people were out of work. By 1933, nearly 13 million were unemployed, or about one out of every four workers. Former businessmen sold apples on the street so they, too, could have money to buy food. People who had lost their homes moved into cardboard shacks. In New York, little

Many people lost their homes in the Great Depression and were forced to settle in shantytowns like this one along the Hudson River in New York.

towns of shanties sprang up along the Hudson River. Times got so rough, quipped Groucho Marx, that "the pigeons started feeding the people in Central Park."

The stock market followed right along. Between the spring of 1930 and the middle of 1932, it spun steadily downward. The Dow Jones Average finally hit bottom on July 8, 1932, at 41.22, a stunning plunge of nearly 90 percent from the September 1929 high. U.S. Steel, which sold for $205 a share at the beginning of the crash, sold for $21.25 in the depths of the Depression. Radio, which climbed above $110 in 1929, fell to a low of $2.50 a share in 1932. The total market value of New York Stock Exchange stocks had been $89.7 billion in September 1929. In July 1932, those stocks had a value of just $15.6 billion.

Looking back from the perspective of the Great Depression, 1929 seemed like a fairy tale, a time of endless promise and prosperity where the ending had somehow turned out all wrong. With the Depression followed by World War II, many people came to believe they would never see that kind of time again. Indeed, it would be November 1954—twenty-five years—before the Dow Jones Industrial Average would again reach the peak it hit in 1929. Nearly forty years would pass before the Stock Exchange would see another 16-million-share day.

Though it wasn't the single cause or even the main cause of the Depression, those six days in October became the turning point, the defining moment, when good times gave way to bad. After the crash, American life would never be the same.

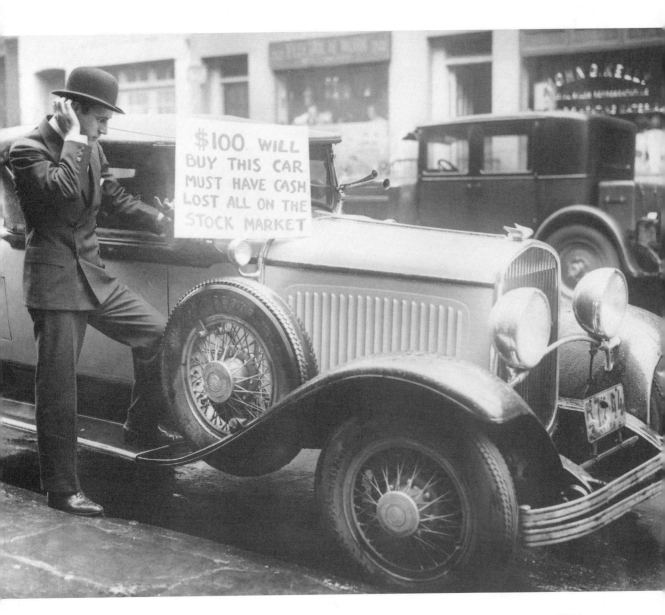

A New York investor named Walter Thorton had to say good-bye to his snazzy car because he desperately needed cash. A man who had stayed out of the stock market quickly bought the roadster.

A New York investor named Walter Thorton had to say good-bye to his snazzy car because he desperately needed cash. A man who had stayed out of the stock market quickly bought the roadster.

EPILOGUE

WHILE THE NATION was desperately concerned about the people out of work, the steep decline in stock prices between 1930 and 1932 and an ongoing banking crisis kept the spotlight on financial institutions.

Distressed by the lows hit in 1932, the Banking and Currency Committee of the United States Senate held two long series of hearings over two years on how the U.S. stock markets worked.

For months, the committee uncovered one grotesque example of greed, abuse, and insider manipulation after another. It exposed how syndicates or pools bid up stock prices; how financial reporters were bribed; the enormously high salaries and bonuses paid to top executives; the special stock deals given to wealthy or influential people. The members grilled Charles E. Mitchell about National City Company's selling of risky, overpriced securities and Albert Wiggin about his profit from betting against Chase National stock—selling short—during the crash. It was, said the fiery Senate prosecutor Ferdinand Pecora, "a shocking disclosure of low standards in high places."

During the hearings in early 1933, Mr. Pecora showed in great detail how National City Company had pushed all kinds of questionable or overpriced stocks and bonds onto unknowing customers. He revealed that the bank had lent one hundred top officers more than $2 million after the crash to help them keep their

Ferdinand Pecora, a tenacious lawyer, led the 1930s investigation into misdeeds on Wall Street during the 1929 crash.

EPILOGUE

WHILE THE NATION was desperately concerned about the people out of work, the steep decline in stock prices between 1930 and 1932 and an ongoing banking crisis kept the spotlight on financial institutions.

Distressed by the lows hit in 1932, the Banking and Currency Committee of the United States Senate held two long series of hearings over two years on how the U.S. stock markets worked.

For months, the committee uncovered one grotesque example of greed, abuse, and insider manipulation after another. It exposed how syndicates or pools bid up stock prices; how financial reporters were bribed; the enormously high salaries and bonuses paid to top executives; the special stock deals given to wealthy or influential people. The members grilled Charles E. Mitchell about National City Company's selling of risky, overpriced securities and Albert Wiggin about his profit from betting against Chase National stock—selling short—during the crash. It was, said the fiery Senate prosecutor Ferdinand Pecora, "a shocking disclosure of low standards in high places."

During the hearings in early 1933, Mr. Pecora showed in great detail how National City Company had pushed all kinds of questionable or overpriced stocks and bonds onto unknowing customers. He revealed that the bank had lent one hundred top officers more than $2 million after the crash to help them keep their

Ferdinand Pecora, a tenacious lawyer, led the 1930s investigation into misdeeds on Wall Street during the 1929 crash.

stocks. Almost none of that money was repaid. The bank was less generous with rank-and-file employ-ees.

Charles E. Mitchell (center) walked confidently from the courthouse after a jury acquitted him of charges that he cheated on his taxes.

In December 1929, when National City stock had slipped to about $200 a share, the bank allowed all employees to buy its shares, with installments to be taken from their paychecks over four years. Though the stock fell to as low as $25 a share, employees still had to pay month after month. The only way to stop the payments was to quit the job in the depths of the Depression.

In the course of his testimony, Mr. Mitchell also admitted that he had sold 18,300 shares of National City to his wife after the crash. The reason? So he could show a loss on the sale that would help him avoid paying taxes.

The many disclosures were so embarrassing to National City and Mr. Mitchell that he resigned soon after his testimony was finished. A month later, he was arrested and charged with illegally cheating the

Albert H. Wiggin (left) testified before a Senate hearing into practices during 1929.
The disclosures during the hearing ruined the long-time banker's reputation.

government out of taxes. A jury found Mr. Mitchell innocent after a six-week trial. Later, he would have to pay additional taxes. After that, even his super-salesmanship skills couldn't erase the belief that the once-powerful banker had lined his own pockets at the expense of many small-time investors.

Albert Wiggin had retired at the end of 1932, after Chase had merged with a Rockefeller bank and Rockefeller men had taken control. In appreciation, the bank had quietly granted him $100,000 a year for life at a time when retirement payments were rare and many people were hungry and out of work. When the payments became public during the hearings in October 1933, many were appalled. Mr. Wiggin voluntarily gave up his pension.

In his testimony, Mr. Wiggin urged the senators to consider how much times had changed in just a few years. "We must not look at things in the year 1933—we cannot look at them now—as we did in 1929," he said. But in 1933, it was hard to warmly recall the giddiness and go-for-it greed of the late 1920s. In addition to his appalling decision to bet against Chase National's stock, Mr. Wiggin had used his private companies to avoid taxes and had overseen a Chase subsidiary that ran a pool in Chase's stock.

Never sorry for his actions, Mr. Wiggin saw his own bank turn against him. The banking company's new chairman, Winthrop W. Aldrich, criticized the bank's old policies and promised a new set of ethics. A newsmagazine had once said, "The Chase is Wiggin and Wiggin is the Chase." But after 1933, the Chase didn't want anything to do with Mr. Wiggin. The bank even sued its former leader over some of his decisions. Mr. Wiggin kept his wealth, but he lost the things he held dearest—respect, prestige, and the support of his beloved company.

Out of the hearings came the first real national rules for the stock market. In a letter to the Senate, President Franklin D. Roosevelt noted, "the Federal Government cannot and should not take any action which might be construed as approving or guaranteeing that newly issued securities are sound in the sense that their value will be maintained or that the properties which they represent will earn a profit." In other words, the government didn't want to get in the business of saying whether any stock was good or bad. But, President Roosevelt said, no important information should be hidden from the buying public. Insiders should not have an edge. "What we seek," he concluded, "is a return to a clearer understanding of the ancient truth that those who manage banks, corporations and other agencies handling or using other people's money are trustees acting for others."

Today, companies must reveal the salaries, bonuses, and other perks paid to their top executives. Executives must disclose the buying and selling they do in their own stocks. Companies must give full explanations of their businesses, their finances, and the risks they face. Secret pools, inside operations, and other market manipulations have been outlawed. The rules cannot keep all companies honest and ethical. But at least now, small investors have some rules to protect them.

For many who had grown up on Wall Street, the old habits were hard to break. One of the first brokers to be accused of violating the new rules was Michael Meehan. In late 1935, the new Securities and Exchange Commission, created to oversee trading practices and information about stocks and bonds, accused Mr. Meehan of improperly trying to increase the price of an inexpensive stock called Bellanca Aircraft. Mr. Meehan denied that he had done anything wrong.

He was heartbroken by the accusation. His family and friends believed the SEC had pounced on Mike Meehan just to make an example out of him. Once genial and upbeat, he turned tense and nervous, and in the summer of 1936, he entered Bloomingdale Hospital, a sanitarium for mental disorders. The next year, after he left the hospital, the SEC expelled him from trading on any American stock exchange. They "took away his real passion," said his grandson Michael Nesbit.

Still, he left a powerful legacy. Business historian John Brooks called Mr. Meehan's handling of Radio's stock "undoubtedly the most spectacular and probably the most disgraceful stock manipulation of the decade." At the same time, he says, Mr. Meehan may have done "more than any one man to make the public love the stock market." The M. J. Meehan firm survived without him and continued as a specialist in a number of major stocks. In 2000, M. J. Meehan, the eighth-largest specialist firm on the New York Stock Exchange, was acquired by FleetBoston Financial Corp.

Shortly after the 1933 hearings, Jack Morgan retired and Thomas Lamont took the reins at J. P. Morgan. New laws required the prestigious financial house to choose between banking and securities. J. P. Morgan continued as a strong and respected bank for

Police took this mug shot of Richard Whitney after he was accused of stealing from his clients.

many years, though changing laws and regulations reduced its power. A new company, Morgan Stanley & Company, was created to take over the securities side of the business. (In 2000, facing a changing world for banking and securities, J. P. Morgan was purchased by Chase Manhattan Corporation, the old Chase Bank.)

Mr. Lamont finished out a distinguished career at Morgan, and continued lecturing and writing until his death in 1948.

Richard Whitney's career took a drastically different turn. Though he appeared to be an astute leader of the New York Stock Exchange, he was an awful investor. Time after time, the stock purchases and other investments he made went bad.

Mr. Whitney served forty months at Sing Sing prison after his conviction for grand larceny. He was paroled in 1941 and barred from ever working on Wall Street again.

Mr. Whitney lost $2 million in the crash and borrowed heavily from his brother George, the Morgan partner. Through much of the 1930s, he made one bad investment after another. To hide his mistakes, he kept borrowing from his brother. But he also began stealing from his customers, and eventually even stole from a special New York Stock Exchange fund. The snobbish Harvard man, who had been a hero in late 1929, turned out to be a common crook.

Caught in 1938, he was convicted of grand theft and sentenced to Sing Sing prison, where he spent three years. The circular Stock Exchange Post 2, given to him in honor of his bid of $205 for Steel, was put up for auction in 1938. It sold for $5.

The crash left Groucho Marx deep in a financial hole. But Groucho still had a good salary, and the Marx Brothers were growing in popularity through both their shows and their movies. As the nation tumbled into economic despair, people needed a good laugh more than ever. The Marx brand of comedy, a biting, cynical kind of humor, was very appealing in a difficult era when ordinary citizens came to distrust government and other authority.

Still, the experience left a permanent mark on Groucho. Worries about money and whether he would continue to be funny and successful kept him awake nights. He developed a ferocious case of insomnia. He tried sleeping on his back, on his stomach, with one pillow and with two, with pajamas and no pajamas, on the bed and on the floor, with a mask and with earplugs. He consulted a psychiatrist. Nothing helped.

Groucho never found a cure, and sleeplessness plagued him the rest of his life. His career dragged in the post-Depression years, but got a second wind in the late 1940s and early 1950s with a hugely successful radio and television game show called *You Bet Your Life*. He also came to terms with the stock market. Despite his losses in the crash, Groucho continued to believe that stocks were a worthwhile way to invest. This time, though, he avoided borrowing and came to rely on a financial adviser he trusted. The man invested cautiously and for the long term. When Groucho went to New York City, he made a point of always visiting his adviser.

Years after the crash, the adviser one day asked Groucho if he would like to see the New York Stock Exchange. It turned out that the comic could neither forgive, nor forget. After watching the trading for a few minutes from the visitors' gallery, Groucho stood up on his chair and began belting out "When Irish Eyes Are Smiling" at the top of his lungs.

The traders stopped their work to look up at the nut in the gallery. They didn't recognize Groucho without his mustache. The adviser tried to stop his friend, saying, "Groucho, I'm afraid they don't appreciate clowning in the Stock Exchange."

But Groucho kept going. A guard told him to be quiet or he would call the police.

"Listen, you crooks," Groucho shouted, now that he had everyone's attention. "You wiped me out of $250,000 in 1929. For that kind of dough, I think I'm entitled to sing if I want to."

Terminally upbeat, Billy Durant stayed in the market through the crash and continued to buy stocks. His ledger books for 1929 show that he sold more shares than he bought and that his brokers sold millions of dollars of stocks when he could not pay his margin debts.

Certain the old magic would return, he continued to play the market in 1930 and lost even more money. He "borrowed" shares from his wife and son, and lost those, too. Brokerage houses sued him to collect their fees for handling his buying and selling. Eventually, the dismal market would wipe out his $100 million in stock winnings—his third and last fortune.

Durant Motors was dissolved in 1933. And after selling most of his property and many of his lifetime possessions, Mr. Durant filed for bankruptcy himself in February 1936 at the age of seventy-four. He listed $900,000 in debts and assets of just $250, his clothes.

He never stopped talking about his return. In letters to the dozens of friends who sent notes sympathizing with his financial situation, he wrote back, "I am enjoying splendid health, my coat is off and sleeves rolled up and am working sixteen hours a day as usual laying the foundation for a comeback. If kind letters from my friends mean anything, I will surely make the grade."

For a time, he owned a food market in New Jersey. Later he returned to Flint, Michigan, where he opened a bowling alley in 1940. By then, his old competitor Henry Ford was a national celebrity, but Mr. Durant was largely forgotten. Despite his years, Mr. Durant talked enthusiastically about bowling becoming a national pastime and laid plans to open a chain of bowling alleys. A stroke put an end to those ideas. Broke and in a wheelchair, he lived out his last years supported by checks sent generously from General Motors men who recognized the legacy he left.

Almost to the end, Billy Durant saw the bright side. "I haven't a dollar, but I'm happy and I'm carrying on because I find I can't stop," he said on his eightieth birthday. "Many people value money too highly," he went on. "After all, money is only loaned to a man; he comes into the world with nothing and he goes out with nothing."

SOURCES,

PICTURE CREDITS,

ACKNOWLEDGMENTS,

AND INDEX

SOURCES

Much of the material in this book is drawn from newspapers and magazines of the day. I relied heavily on news accounts in *The New York Times,* the New York *World,* and *The Wall Street Journal,* as well as the *New York Daily News, New York Herald Tribune, New York American, New York Telegram,* and the *New York Sun.* Some stories and details also came from *Time, Newsweek, Literary Digest,* and the *Saturday Evening Post.*

In addition, this account reflects throughout the work of the following writers about the Crash and the times:

Allen, Frederick Lewis. *Only Yesterday: An Informal History of the Nineteen-Twenties.* New York: Harper & Row, 1931, 1964.

Brooks, John. *Once in Golconda: A True Drama of Wall Street, 1920-1938.* New York: John Wiley & Sons, 1969; 2nd ed., 1999.

Galbraith, John Kenneth. *The Great Crash 1929.* Boston: Houghton Mifflin Company, 1954; 2nd ed., 1997.

Thomas, Gordon, and Max Morgan-Witts. *The Day the Bubble Burst: A Social History of the Wall Street Crash of 1929.* Garden City, N.Y.: Doubleday & Company, 1979.

Sparling, Earl. *Mystery Men of Wall Street: The Powers Behind the Market.* New York: Greenberg, 1930.

Whitney, Richard. "The Work of the New York Stock Exchange in the Panic of 1929." Address delivered to the Boston Association of Stock Exchange Firms, June 10, 1930. This speech can be found in several forms, including in *Anatomy of a Crash* by J. R. Levian. New York: Traders Press, 1966.

Other valuable sources are listed below in the chapter where the information appears.

INTRODUCTION

Kennedy, David M. *Freedom from Fear: The American People in Depression and War, 1929-1945.* New York: Oxford University Press, 1999.

Sobel, Robert. *The Big Board: A History of the New York Stock Market.* New York: The Free Press, 1965.

Soule, George. *Prosperity Decade: A Chapter from American Economic History, 1917-1929.* London: Pilot Press Limited, 1947.

BLACK THURSDAY

Lefevre, Edwin. "The Little Fellow in Wall Street." *The Saturday Evening Post,* 4 January 1930, 6–7, 97, 100, 102, 105.

SELL!

Buck, James E., ed. *The New York Stock Exchange: the First 200 Years*. Essex, Conn.: Greenwich Publishing Group, 1992.

Knapp, Paul. *The Berengaria Exchange: The Lively Account of a Floating Stock Exchange During the Fateful Week of the 1929 Crash*. New York: Dial Press, 1972.

Marx, Arthur. *Life with Groucho*. New York: Simon & Schuster, 1954.

Meehan, Terence S. Interview by author. June 2000.

Meeker, J. Edward. *The Work of the Stock Exchange*. New York: Ronald Press, 1930.

Nesbit, Michael. Interview by author. June 2000.

Radio Corporation of America annual reports for 1928 and 1929, and RCA promotional materials from the collection of the Hagley Museum, Wilmington, Del.

Sparling, Earl. "These Brokers." *Scribners* (July 1930): 18–24.

WHITE KNIGHTS TO THE RESCUE

Brooklyn Daily Eagle, 25 October 1929, clipping from J. P. Morgan archives.

Cockburn, Claud. *In Time of Trouble, An Autobiography*. London: Rupert Hart-Davis, 1957.

Josephson, Matthew. *The Money Lords: The Great Finance Capitalists 1929-1950* and *Infidel in the Temple: A Memoir of the Nineteen-Thirties*. New York: Weybright and Talley, 1972.

Lamont, Edward M. *The Ambassador from Wall Street: The Story of Thomas W. Lamont, J. P. Morgan's Chief Executive*. Lanham, Md.: Madison Books, 1994.

Lamont, Thomas W. Speeches from the J. P. Morgan & Co. archives.

Pilpel, Robert H. *Churchill in America, 1895-1961: An Affectionate Portrait*. New York: Harcourt Brace Jovanovich, 1976.

PRESIDENT HOOVER RESPONDS

Anonymous. "Now I've Gone Back to Work." *American Magazine,* February 1930, 31, 86–89.

Hoover, Herbert. *The Memoirs of Herbert Hoover, Vol. 3, The Great Depression 1929-1941*. New York: The Macmillan Company, 1952.

Meeker. *The Work of the Stock Exchange.*

New York Stock Exchange Bulletin (January 1933): 1.

Stock Exchange Practices. Hearings before the Committee on Banking and Currency, U.S. Senate, 73rd Congress, testimony of Otto H. Kahn and Exhibit 92, February 24, 1934.

SOLD OUT

"Animal Crackers at Maryland." *Baltimore Sunday Sun,* 27 October 1929.

Cantor, Eddie. *Caught Short! A Saga of Wailing Wall Street*. New York: Simon & Schuster, 1929.

Kanour, Gilbert. "Animal Crackers at The Maryland." *Baltimore Evening Sun,* 30 October 1929.

Kirkley, Donald. "Understudy Gets Another Chance Here." *Baltimore Sunday Sun,* 3 November 1929, sec. 2.

Klingaman, William K. *1929: The Year of the Great Crash*. New York: Harper & Row, 1989.

Marx, A. *Life with Groucho.*

"Marx Brothers at Maryland in 'Animal Crackers.'" *Baltimore Sun,* 29 October 1929.

Marx, Groucho. *Groucho and Me: The Autobiography of Groucho Marx*. New York: Bernard Geis Associates, 1959.

Marx, Harpo, with Rowland Barber. *Harpo Speaks!* New York: Limelight Editions, 1985.

THE KING OF THE BULLS

Durant, William C., Papers. Scharchburg Archives, Kettering University, Flint, Mich.

Flynn, John T. "Riders of the Whirlwind." *Collier's*, 19 January 1929. Scharchburg Archives, Kettering University, Flint, Mich.

Gustin, Lawrence R. *Billy Durant: Creator of General Motors*. Grand Rapids, Mich.: William B. Eerdmans, 1973.

Newmark, J. H. "My 25 Years with W. C. Durant." *Commerce and Finance* (16 May 1936): 344–346; (30 May 1936): 380–382, 403; (13 June 1936): 420–422; (27 June 1936): 454–456; (11 July 1936): 492–494; (25 July 1936): 532–534; (8 August 1936): 568–570; (22 August 1936): 606–608; (5 September 1936): 644–646; (19 September 1936): 678–680; (3 October 1936): 720–722; (17 October 1936): 756–758.

Weisberger, Bernard A. *The Dream Maker: William C. Durant, Founder of General Motors*. Boston: Little, Brown & Co., 1979.

A BLOODY MONDAY

Pecora, Ferdinand. *Wall Street Under Oath: The Story of our Modern Money Changers*. New York: Simon & Schuster, 1939. Reprinted by Augustus M. Kelley, Publishers, New York, 1968.

Prescott, Marjorie Wiggin. *New England Son*. New York: Dodd Mead and Company, 1949.

Stock Exchange Practices. Hearings before the Committee on Banking and Currency, U.S. Senate, 73rd Congress, testimony of Albert H. Wiggin, November 1, 1933.

BLACK TUESDAY

Josephson, Matthew. "Groton, Harvard, Wall Street." *The New Yorker,* 2 April 1932, 19–22.

New York Stock Exchange Year Book, 1929-1930, pp. 78–79.

Pilpel. *Churchill in America*.

Thomas and Morgan-Witts. *The Day the Bubble Burst*.

AFTERMATH

Anonymous. "Now I've Gone Back to Work," *American Magazine,* February 1930, 31.

Cantor. *Caught Short! A Saga of Wailing Wall Street*.

Lamont. *The Ambassador from Wall Street*.

Marx with Barber. *Harpo Speaks!*

Nesbit, Michael. Interview by author. June 2000.

New York Stock Exchange Bulletin (May 1932): 1.

New York Stock Exchange Report of the President, 1 May 1929–1 May 1930.

Patterson, Robert T. *The Great Boom and Panic, 1921-1929*. Chicago: Henry Regnery Co., 1965.

EPILOGUE

Durant, William C. Papers. Scharchburg Archives, Kettering University, Flint, Mich.

Legislative History of The Securities Act of 1933 and Securities Exchange Act of 1934. Compiled by J. S. Ellenberger and Ellen P. Maher. South Hackensack, N.J.: Fred B. Rothman & Co. for the Law Librarians Society of Washington, D.C., 1973.

Marx, G. *Groucho and Me*.

Marx, A. *Life with Groucho*.

Nesbit, Michael. Interview by author. June 2000.

Pecora. *Wall Street Under Oath*.

Stock Exchange Practices. Hearings before the Committee on Banking and Currency, U.S. Senate, 73rd Congress, testimony of Albert H. Wiggin (October 17, 27, and 31, 1933; November 1 and 2, 1933) and Otto H. Kahn (June 29–30, 1933).

PICTURE CREDITS

Every effort has been made to trace the copyright holders, and we apologize for any unintentional omissions. We would be pleased to insert the appropriate acknowledgment in any subsequent editions of this book.

p. 97: AP/Wide World Photos

p. 98: Brown Brothers

p. 99: From the Museum of American Financial History, reproduced from *The Magazine of Business*. Used with permission of the Science, Industry & Business Library, New York Public Library, Astor, Lenox and Tilden Foundations

p. 100: New York Stock Exchange

p. 102: Brown Brothers

p. 105: *New York Daily News*

p. 109: *New York Daily News*

p. 111: *Wall Street Journal,* 2 November 1929, p. 12

p. 116: New York Stock Exchange

p. 119: *Wall Street Journal,* 1 November 1929, p. 2

pp. 120, 121: New York Stock Exchange

p. 125: © Bettman/CORBIS

p. 127: Time Inc.

p. 130: The New-York Historical Society

p. 133: The New-York Historical Society

p. 135: © Bettman/CORBIS

p. 138: © Bettman/CORBIS

p. 139: © Bettman/CORBIS

p. 140: *New York Daily News*

p. 143: AP/Wide World Photos

p. 144: © Bettman/CORBIS

ACKNOWLEDGMENTS

GRATEFUL THANKS are due to the following for opening up their resources, helping me with research or offering much-appreciated guidance on pulling this all together.

Steven Wheeler, New York Stock Exchange archivist

Bill Holleran, former curator, Scharchburg Archives, Kettering University, Flint, Michigan

Shelly Diamond, Chase Manhattan archives

David W. Wright, J. P. Morgan & Co. archives

Christi Harlan, former communications director, and Joseph R. Kolinski, chief clerk, U.S. Senate Committee on Banking, Housing, and Urban Affairs

Terence S. Meehan, M. J. Meehan & Co.

Michael Nesbit, M. J. Meehan & Co.

Meg Ventrudo, Museum of American Financial History

Emily Nelson

Carlos Tejada

Museum of the City of New York

New-York Historical Society

Hagley Museum and Library

My wonderful family: Scott McCartney, Abby McCartney, and Jenny McCartney

Doug Sease and Steve Adler of *The Wall Street Journal*

Virginia Skrelja and Brenda Bowen of Simon & Schuster

..1932 Lows...Dow: 41.22...ATT: 70.25...GM: 7.63...Radio: 2.50...Steel: 21.25...1932 Lows...D

Index